Take a trip from sea to shining sea with this outrageous atlas. You'll find spectac... spots under the spacious skies, freaky facts from the fruited plains, peculiar points of t... purple mountains majesty, and amazing info about those amber waves of grain. It's America the beautiful — land of the free and home of the strange!

TABLE OF CONTENTS

Design and Illustrations by Dave Winter

Researched, written and produced by Davidson Marketing, Inc., Chicago, Illinois.

WARNING: *We're pretty darn sure the facts you are about to read are facts, but some are rooted in folklore. So don't blame us if the world's biggest ball of string isn't the world's biggest anymore.*

Most atlases do not place New York and Ohio in these regions. We did it because we are not most atlases and it made our job a heck of a lot easier. If we confused you or your parents, get over it.

UNITED STATES
PACIFIC OCEAN
Pacific Coast Highway
CANADA
UNITED STATES
WASHINGTON
Bellingham
NORTH CASCADES NAT. PK.
Port Angeles
OLYMPIC NAT. PK.
Everett
Seattle
Coulee Dam
Tacoma
OLYMPIA
MT. RAINIER
Yakima
Longview
Spokane
Coeur d'Alene
OREGON
Portland
SALEM
CASCADE
CRATER LAKE NAT. PK.
Medford
BOISE
IDAHO
Snake R.
Idaho Falls
Pocatello
MONTANA
Missoula
Great Falls
HELENA
Butte
Billings
Peck Lake
NORTH DAKOTA
Minot
Grand Forks
T. ROOSEVELT NAT. PK.
BISMARCK
Lake Sakakawea
SOUTH DAKOTA
Lake Oahe
Aberdeen
PIERRE
Rapid City
BADLANDS NAT. PK.
WIND CAVE NAT. PK.
VOTE
YELLOWSTONE NAT. PK.
Cody
GRAND TETON NAT. PK.
WYOMING
Casper
CHEYENNE
FLAMING GORGE NAT. REC. AREA
NEBRASKA
North Platte
Oregon Trail
REDWOOD NAT. PK.
Weed
Eureka
Redding
LASSEN VOLCANIC NAT. PK.
SIERRA NEVADA
Reno
Lake Tahoe
CARSON CITY
SACRAMENTO
Stockton
San Francisco
Oakland
San Jose
Modesto
Merced
YOSEMITE NAT. PK.
Monterey
Salinas
KINGS CANYON NAT. PK.
Fresno
SEQUOIA NAT. PK.
Mt. Whitney 14494
DEATH VALLEY
CALIFORNIA
Santa Maria
Santa Barbara
HOLLYWOOD
Glendale
Los Angeles
San Bernardino
Santa Ana
CHANNEL ISLANDS NAT. PK.
MOJAVE DESERT
NEVADA
Elko
Las Vegas
Lake Mead
Hoover Dam
LAKE MEAD NAT. REC. AREA
Great Salt Lake
GREAT SALT LAKE DESERT
Ogden
SALT LAKE CITY
Provo
UTAH
CAPITOL REEF NAT. PK.
CANYONLANDS NAT. PK.
ARCHES NAT. PK.
ZION NAT. PK.
BRYCE CANYON NAT. PK.
Lake Powell
GLEN CANYON NAT. REC. AREA
GRAND CANYON NAT. PK.
Grand Canyon
Flagstaff
ARIZONA
PETRIFIED FOR. NAT. PK.
PHOENIX
Tucson
Nogales
UNITED STATES
MEXICO
COLORADO
Grand Junction
Boulder
DENVER
Colorado Springs
Pueblo
MESA VERDE NAT. PK.
Gallup
SANTA FE
Albuquerque
NEW MEXICO
Rio Grande
Roswell
White Sands
Las Cruces
El Paso
Ciudad Juárez
CARLSBAD CAVERNS NAT. PK.
Carlsbad
GUADALUPE MTS. NAT. PK.
KANSAS
Dodge City
OKLAHOMA CITY
Amarillo
Lawton
Red R.
Lubbock
Wichita Falls
OK
Fort Worth
Abilene
Midland
Odessa
TEXAS
BIG BEND NAT. PK.
PRESA DE LA AMISTAD
Eagle Pass
San Antonio
Laredo
Falcon Dam
McAllen
HAWAII
KAUAI
Kapaa
Lihue
Waimea
OAHU
Kailua
Wahiawa
HONOLULU
MOLOKAI
Kaunakakai
Wailuku
MAUI
Lanai
Hilo
Mauna Kea
HAWAII
Mauna Loa
Pahoa
HAWAII VOLCANOES NAT. PK.
Barrow
Pt. Hope
BROOKS RANGE
Prudhoe Bay
KOBUK VALLEY NAT. PK.
GATES OF THE ARCTIC NAT. PK.
Kotzebue
Gambell
Nome
ALASKA
Fort Yukon
Fairbanks
Eagle
Mt. McKinley
DENALI NAT. PK.
Bethel
Delta
Tok
Anchorage
Palmer
Valdez
Cordova
WRANGELL ST. ELIAS NAT. PK.
Mt. St. Elias
Seward
ALASKA PENINSULA
KODIAK I.
Skagway
Haines
JUNEAU
GLACIER BAY
Ketchikan
MISTY FJORDS
CANADA
UNITED STATES

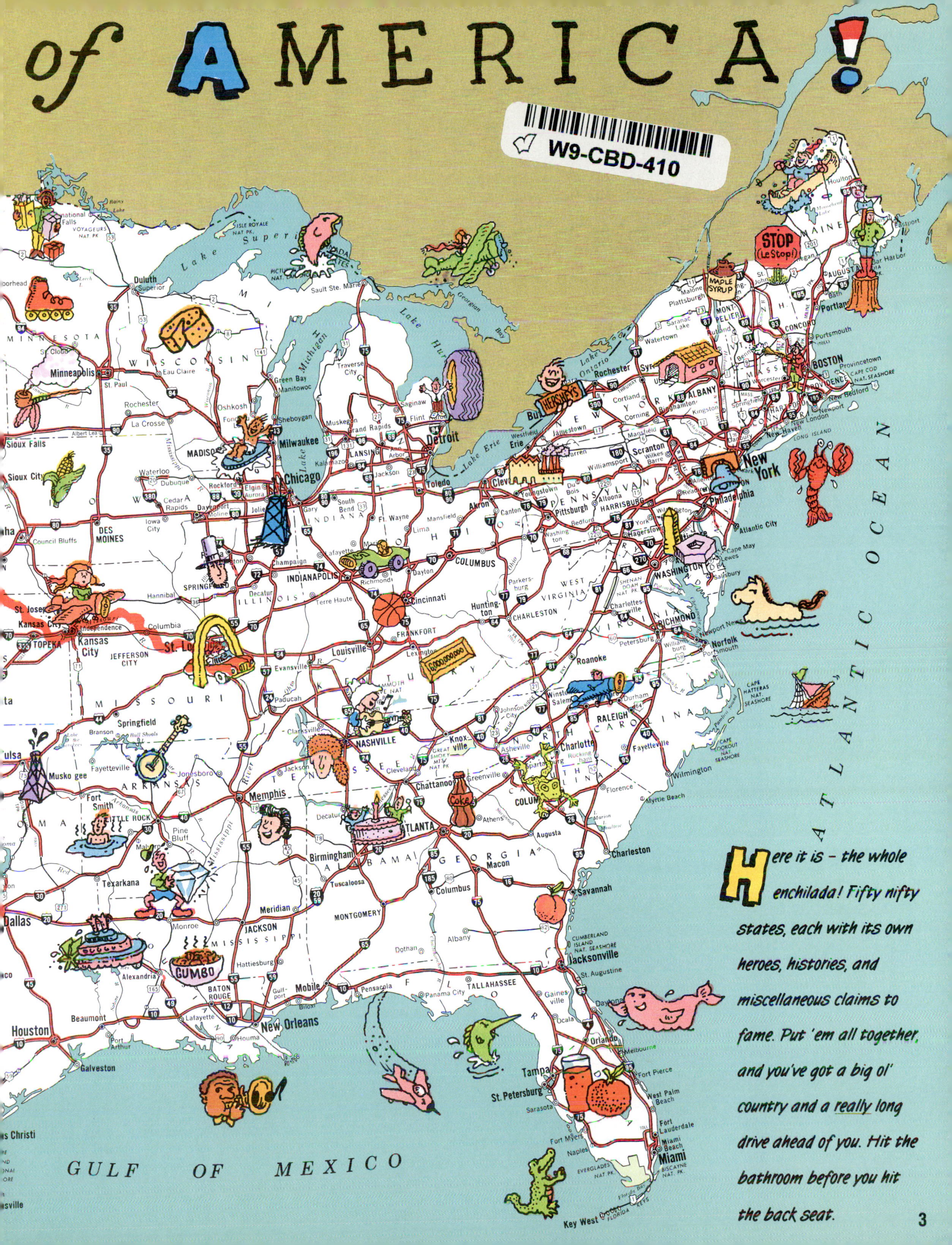
of AMERICA!
GULF OF MEXICO
ATLANTIC OCEAN
Lake Superior
Lake Michigan
Lake Huron
Lake Erie
Lake Ontario
MINNESOTA
WISCONSIN
IOWA
ILLINOIS
INDIANA
OHIO
MISSOURI
KENTUCKY
TENNESSEE
ARKANSAS
MISSISSIPPI
ALABAMA
GEORGIA
FLORIDA
NORTH CAROLINA
SOUTH CAROLINA
VIRGINIA
WEST VIRGINIA
PENNSYLVANIA
NEW YORK
MAINE
CANADA
Chicago
Detroit
New York
Philadelphia
Boston
WASHINGTON
New Orleans
Houston
Dallas
Miami
ATLANTA
NASHVILLE
Memphis
Minneapolis
Kansas City
St. Louis
Louisville
Cincinnati
COLUMBUS
Pittsburgh
RICHMOND
Charlotte
Jacksonville
Tampa
STOP (Le Stop!)
MAPLE SYRUP
HERSHEY'S
GUMBO
Coke
Here it is – the whole enchilada! Fifty nifty states, each with its own heroes, histories, and miscellaneous claims to fame. Put 'em all together, and you've got a big ol' country and a really long drive ahead of you. Hit the bathroom before you hit the back seat.

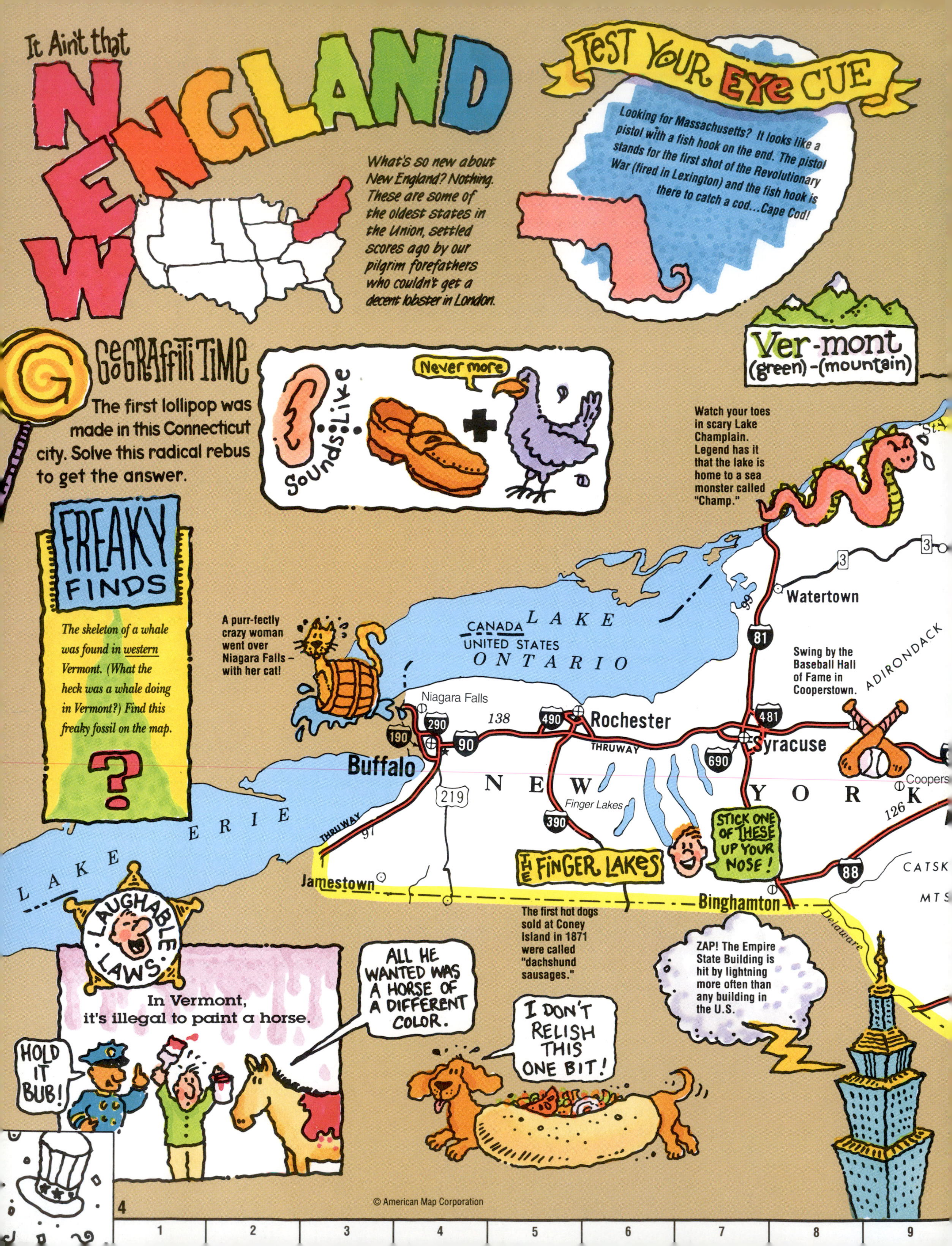

It Ain't that
NEW ENGLAND
What's so new about New England? Nothing. These are some of the oldest states in the Union, settled scores ago by our pilgrim forefathers who couldn't get a decent lobster in London.
TEST YOUR EYE CUE
Looking for Massachusetts? It looks like a pistol with a fish hook on the end. The pistol stands for the first shot of the Revolutionary War (fired in Lexington) and the fish hook is there to catch a cod...Cape Cod!
Ver-mont
(green)-(mountain)
GeOGRAffiTi TIME
The first lollipop was made in this Connecticut city. Solve this radical rebus to get the answer.
Sounds:Like
Never more
FREAKY FINDS
The skeleton of a whale was found in western Vermont. (What the heck was a whale doing in Vermont?) Find this freaky fossil on the map.
?
Watch your toes in scary Lake Champlain. Legend has it that the lake is home to a sea monster called "Champ."
A purr-fectly crazy woman went over Niagara Falls – with her cat!
Swing by the Baseball Hall of Fame in Cooperstown.
CANADA
UNITED STATES
LAKE ONTARIO
LAKE ERIE
NEW YORK
ADIRONDACK
CATSK
MTS
Watertown
Niagara Falls
Rochester
Syracuse
Buffalo
Jamestown
Binghamton
Coopers
Finger Lakes
Delaware
THRUWAY
3
81
481
690
490
290
190
90
138
219
390
97
126
88
THE FINGER LAKES
STICK ONE OF THESE UP YOUR NOSE!
The first hot dogs sold at Coney Island in 1871 were called "dachshund sausages."
ZAP! The Empire State Building is hit by lightning more often than any building in the U.S.
LAUGHABLE LAWS
In Vermont, it's illegal to paint a horse.
HOLD IT BUB!
ALL HE WANTED WAS A HORSE OF A DIFFERENT COLOR.
I DON'T RELISH THIS ONE BIT!
© American Map Corporation
1 2 3 4 5 6 7 8 9

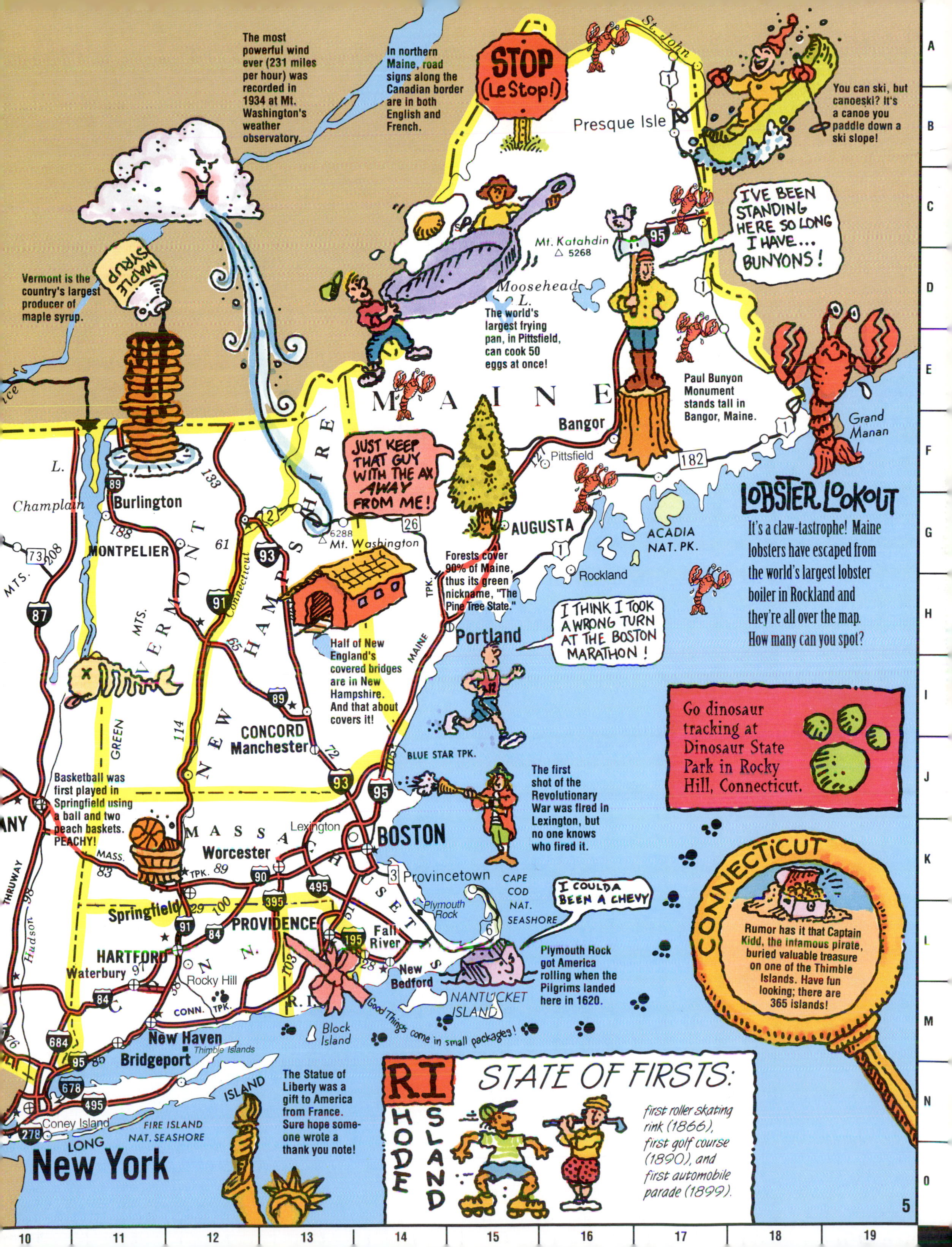

The most powerful wind ever (231 miles per hour) was recorded in 1934 at Mt. Washington's weather observatory.
In northern Maine, road signs along the Canadian border are in both English and French.
STOP (Le Stop!)
St. John
Presque Isle
You can ski, but canoeski? It's a canoe you paddle down a ski slope!
I'VE BEEN STANDING HERE SO LONG I HAVE... BUNYONS!
MAPLE SYRUP
Vermont is the country's largest producer of maple syrup.
Mt. Katahdin 5268
Moosehead L.
The world's largest frying pan, in Pittsfield, can cook 50 eggs at once!
Paul Bunyon Monument stands tall in Bangor, Maine.
MAINE
Bangor
Pittsfield
Grand Manan
JUST KEEP THAT GUY WITH THE AX AWAY FROM ME!
AUGUSTA
NEW HAMPSHIRE
6288 Mt. Washington
L. Champlain
Burlington
MONTPELIER
VERMONT
GREEN MTS.
Connecticut
ACADIA NAT. PK.
Rockland
LOBSTER LOOKOUT
It's a claw-tastrophe! Maine lobsters have escaped from the world's largest lobster boiler in Rockland and they're all over the map. How many can you spot?
Forests cover 90% of Maine, thus its green nickname, "The Pine Tree State."
I THINK I TOOK A WRONG TURN AT THE BOSTON MARATHON!
Portland
MAINE TPK.
Half of New England's covered bridges are in New Hampshire. And that about covers it!
CONCORD
Manchester
BLUE STAR TPK.
Go dinosaur tracking at Dinosaur State Park in Rocky Hill, Connecticut.
Basketball was first played in Springfield using a ball and two peach baskets. PEACHY!
The first shot of the Revolutionary War was fired in Lexington, but no one knows who fired it.
Lexington
BOSTON
MASSACHUSETTS
Worcester
MASS. TPK.
Provincetown
CAPE COD NAT. SEASHORE
I COULDA BEEN A CHEVY
Plymouth Rock
Springfield
PROVIDENCE
Fall River
New Bedford
HARTFORD
Waterbury
Rocky Hill
CONN. TPK.
R.I.
Plymouth Rock got America rolling when the Pilgrims landed here in 1620.
NANTUCKET ISLAND
CONNECTICUT
Rumor has it that Captain Kidd, the infamous pirate, buried valuable treasure on one of the Thimble Islands. Have fun looking; there are 365 islands!
Block Island
Good Things come in small packages!
New Haven
Bridgeport
Thimble Islands
THRUWAY
Hudson
LONG ISLAND
Coney Island
FIRE ISLAND NAT. SEASHORE
New York
The Statue of Liberty was a gift to America from France. Sure hope someone wrote a thank you note!
RI RHODE ISLAND
STATE OF FIRSTS:
first roller skating rink (1866), first golf course (1890), and first automobile parade (1899).

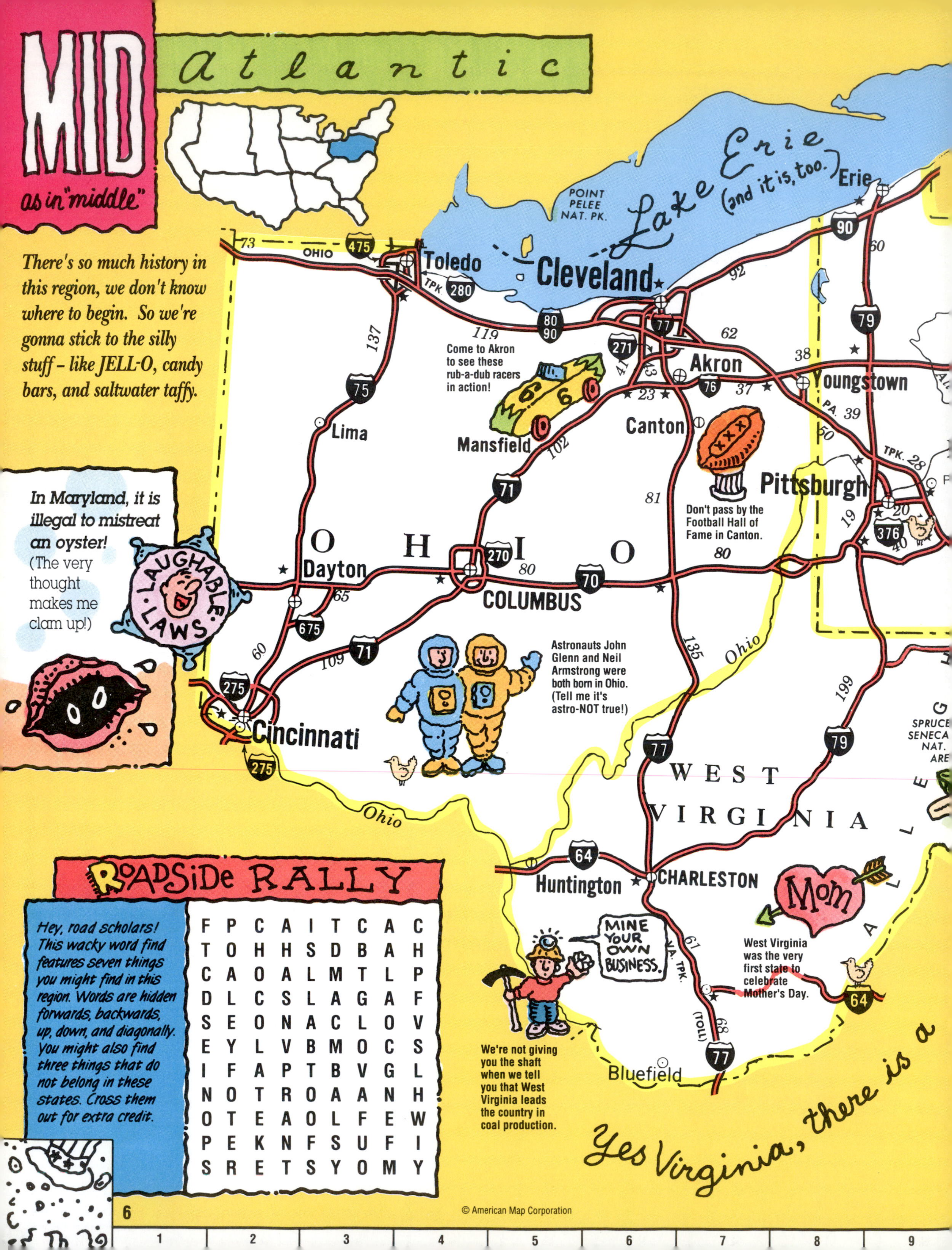

MID atlantic
as in "middle"
There's so much history in this region, we don't know where to begin. So we're gonna stick to the silly stuff – like JELL-O, candy bars, and saltwater taffy.
In Maryland, it is illegal to mistreat an oyster! (The very thought makes me clam up!)
LAUGHABLE LAWS
Lake Erie (and it is, too.)
POINT PELEE NAT. PK.
Erie
Toledo
Cleveland
OHIO
TPK
Come to Akron to see these rub-a-dub racers in action!
Akron
Youngstown
Lima
Mansfield
Canton
Pittsburgh
Don't pass by the Football Hall of Fame in Canton.
O H I O
Dayton
COLUMBUS
Astronauts John Glenn and Neil Armstrong were both born in Ohio. (Tell me it's astro-NOT true!)
Cincinnati
Ohio
WEST VIRGINIA
SPRUCE SENECA NAT. ARE
Huntington
CHARLESTON
MINE YOUR OWN BUSINESS.
Mom
West Virginia was the very first state to celebrate Mother's Day.
We're not giving you the shaft when we tell you that West Virginia leads the country in coal production.
VA. TPK.
(TOLL)
Bluefield
Yes Virginia, there is a
ROADSIDE RALLY
Hey, road scholars! This wacky word find features seven things you might find in this region. Words are hidden forwards, backwards, up, down, and diagonally. You might also find three things that do not belong in these states. Cross them out for extra credit.
F P C A I T C A C
T O H H S D B A H
C A O A L M T L P
D L C S L A G A F
S E O N A C L O V
E Y L V B M O C S
I F A P T B V G L
N O T R O A A N H
O T E A O L F E W
P E K N F S U F I
S R E T S Y O M Y

1 2 3 4 5 6 7 8 9

MAP
a
n
i
a
Legend has it (map legend, that is) there are lots of historical monuments throughout this region of the country. What's a legend? A legend is a story, but a legend is also an explanation for symbols on a map. Look for the historic monuments (marked with red dots) on this map. Hint: the Liberty Bell is one. Can you find two more?
I'VE BEEN SEWING SO LONG I'M SEEING STARS!
Betsy Ross sewed the first American flag in Pennsylvania.
Hershey, Pennsylvania is home sweet home to the Great American Chocolate Bar.
HERSHEY'S
Ben Franklin made his electrifying discovery outside Philadelphia!
Abe's famous Gettysburg Address was a tribute to the 50,000 men who died during the Civil War's biggest battle.
This Baltimore babe is better known as the Sultan of Swat. It's Babe Ruth!
Washington Monument
"The Star Spangled Banner," inspired by the flag waving on top of Fort McHenry, went on to TOP the charts.
Here's a sticky fact: Atlantic City is the saltwater taffy capital of the world. Sea water drenched a taffy vendor's stand and that's how it got its name!
Log cabins come from Sweden, but the first one in America was built in Delaware.
ASSATEAGUE I. NAT. SEASHORE
Here's a real pony tale: There are still wild ponies on Assateague Island!
Hold still!
What wiggles, squishes, tastes fruity, and was first made in Delaware? JELL-O!
Ride the Potomac River at the National Kayak Championships.
VIRGINIA! (try page 9)
GROUSE ME OUT!
Pennsylvania's state bird is the Ruffled Grouse...and there are five of them hidden on this map. Find them.
Hint: some of them may have left Pennsylvania.
PENNSYLVANIA
APPALACHIAN MTS.
MARYLAND
DEL.
NEW JERSEY
Scranton
Newark
Allentown
TRENTON
Liberty Bell
HARRISBURG
Hershey
Gettysburg
Philadelphia
Camden
Wilmington
Baltimore
Ft. McHenry
ANNAPOLIS
WASHINGTON
Pentagon
Atlantic City
Cumberland
Delaware
Potomac
Chesapeake Bay
N. E. EX PA. TPK.
PENNSYLVANIA TPK.
ATLANTIC CITY EXPY.
GARDEN STATE PKY.
FT. MCHENRY
A B C D E F G H I J K L M N O
10 11 12 13 14 15 16 17 18 19

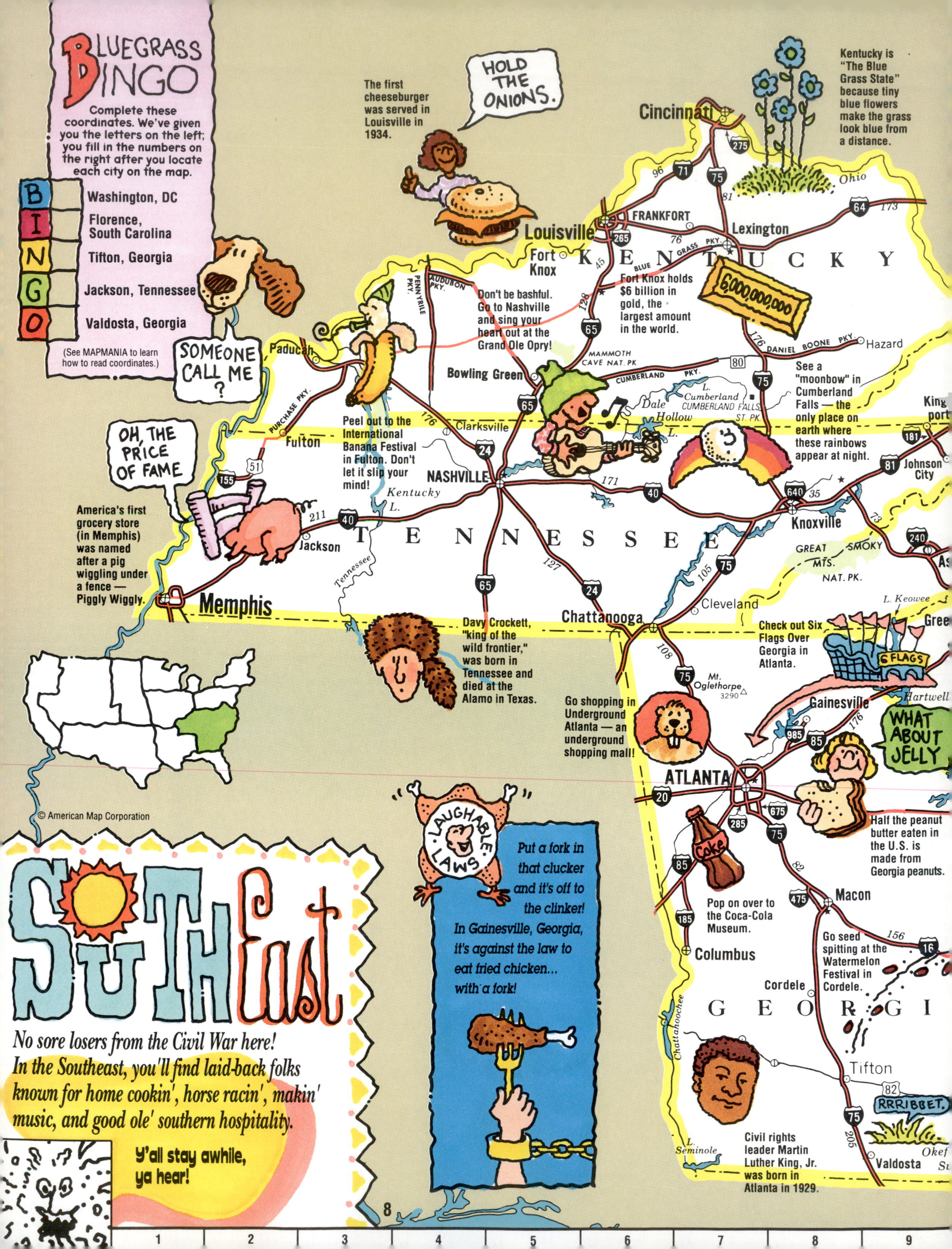

BLUEGRASS BINGO
Complete these coordinates. We've given you the letters on the left; you fill in the numbers on the right after you locate each city on the map.
B Washington, DC
I Florence, South Carolina
N Tifton, Georgia
G Jackson, Tennessee
O Valdosta, Georgia
(See MAPMANIA to learn how to read coordinates.)
SOMEONE CALL ME ?
OH, THE PRICE OF FAME
America's first grocery store (in Memphis) was named after a pig wiggling under a fence — Piggly Wiggly.
© American Map Corporation
The first cheeseburger was served in Louisville in 1934.
HOLD THE ONIONS.
Don't be bashful. Go to Nashville and sing your heart out at the Grand Ole Opry!
Peel out to the International Banana Festival in Fulton. Don't let it slip your mind!
Kentucky is "The Blue Grass State" because tiny blue flowers make the grass look blue from a distance.
Fort Knox holds $6 billion in gold, the largest amount in the world.
6,000,000,000
See a "moonbow" in Cumberland Falls — the only place on earth where these rainbows appear at night.
Davy Crockett, "king of the wild frontier," was born in Tennessee and died at the Alamo in Texas.
Go shopping in Underground Atlanta — an underground shopping mall!
Check out Six Flags Over Georgia in Atlanta.
6 FLAGS
WHAT ABOUT JELLY
Half the peanut butter eaten in the U.S. is made from Georgia peanuts.
Pop on over to the Coca-Cola Museum.
Coke
Go seed spitting at the Watermelon Festival in Cordele.
RRRIBBET.
Civil rights leader Martin Luther King, Jr. was born in Atlanta in 1929.
LAUGHABLE LAWS
Put a fork in that clucker and it's off to the clinker! In Gainesville, Georgia, it's against the law to eat fried chicken... with a fork!
Cincinnati
Ohio
FRANKFORT
Louisville
Lexington
Fort Knox
KENTUCKY
BLUE GRASS PKY.
AUDUBON PKY.
PENNYRILE PKY.
MAMMOTH CAVE NAT. PK
DANIEL BOONE PKY.
Hazard
Paducah
Bowling Green
CUMBERLAND PKY.
L. Cumberland
CUMBERLAND FALLS ST. PK.
Dale Hollow L.
PURCHASE PKY.
Fulton
Clarksville
NASHVILLE
Kentucky L.
Kingsport
Johnson City
Knoxville
GREAT SMOKY MTS. NAT. PK.
Jackson
TENNESSEE
Tennessee
Memphis
Chattanooga
Cleveland
L. Keowee
Mt. Oglethorpe 3290
Gainesville
Hartwell
ATLANTA
Macon
Columbus
Cordele
GEORGIA
Chattahoochee
Tifton
L. Seminole
Valdosta
SOUTHEast
No sore losers from the Civil War here! In the Southeast, you'll find laid-back folks known for home cookin', horse racin', makin' music, and good ole' southern hospitality.
Y'all stay awhile, ya hear!
8
1 2 3 4 5 6 7 8 9

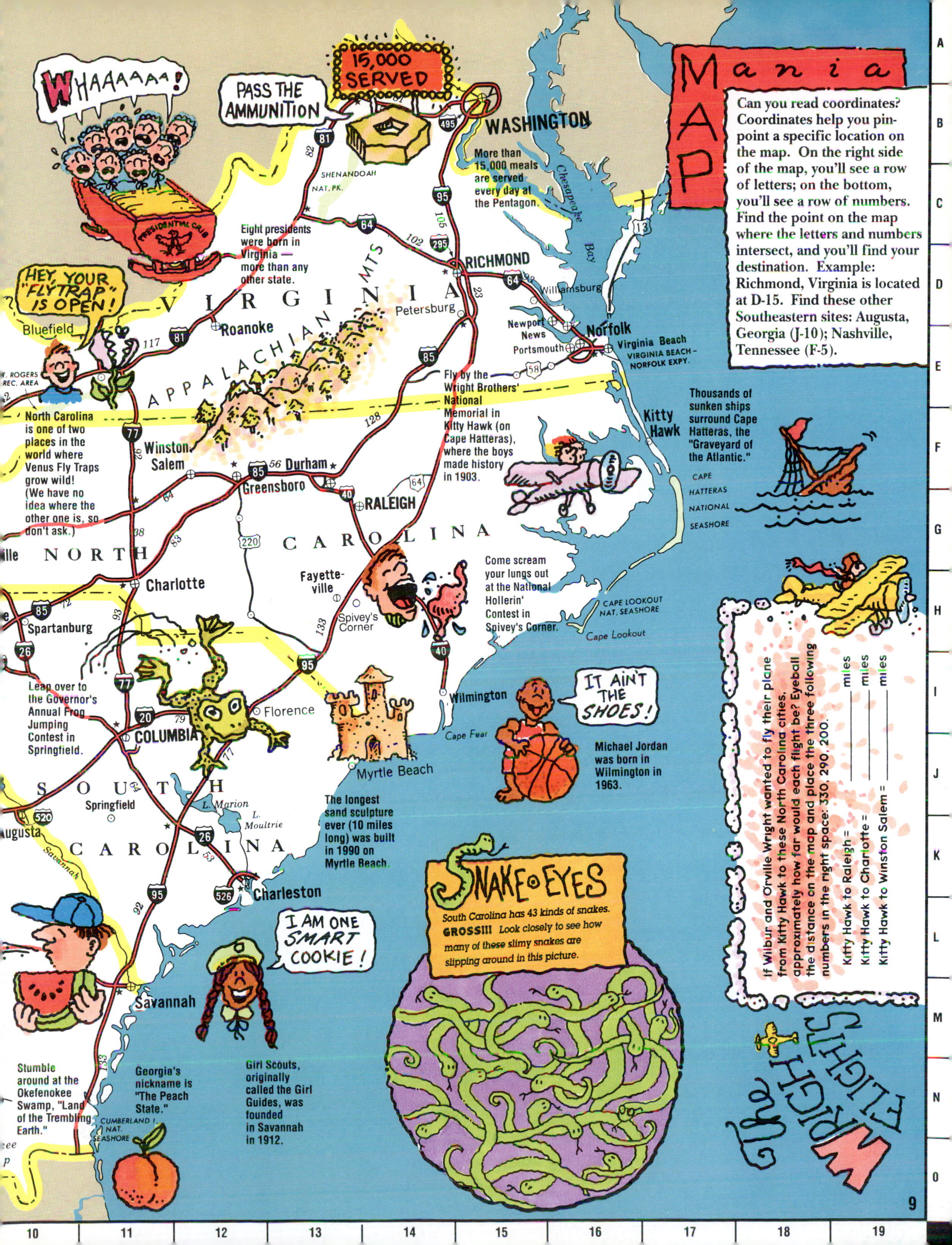

Map Mania
Can you read coordinates? Coordinates help you pinpoint a specific location on the map. On the right side of the map, you'll see a row of letters; on the bottom, you'll see a row of numbers. Find the point on the map where the letters and numbers intersect, and you'll find your destination. Example: Richmond, Virginia is located at D-15. Find these other Southeastern sites: Augusta, Georgia (J-10); Nashville, Tennessee (F-5).
WHAAAAAA!
PRESIDENTIAL CAR
PASS THE AMMUNITION
15,000 SERVED
WASHINGTON
More than 15,000 meals are served every day at the Pentagon.
SHENANDOAH NAT. PK.
Chesapeake Bay
Eight presidents were born in Virginia — more than any other state.
RICHMOND
Williamsburg
Petersburg
Newport News
Portsmouth
Norfolk
Virginia Beach
VIRGINIA BEACH-NORFOLK EXPY.
HEY, YOUR "FLYTRAP" IS OPEN!
Bluefield
VIRGINIA
APPALACHIAN MTS
Roanoke
North Carolina is one of two places in the world where Venus Fly Traps grow wild! (We have no idea where the other one is, so don't ask.)
Fly by the Wright Brothers' National Memorial in Kitty Hawk (on Cape Hatteras), where the boys made history in 1903.
Kitty Hawk
Thousands of sunken ships surround Cape Hatteras, the "Graveyard of the Atlantic."
CAPE HATTERAS NATIONAL SEASHORE
Winston-Salem
Durham
Greensboro
RALEIGH
NORTH CAROLINA
Charlotte
Fayetteville
Spivey's Corner
Come scream your lungs out at the National Hollerin' Contest in Spivey's Corner.
CAPE LOOKOUT NAT. SEASHORE
Cape Lookout
Spartanburg
Leap over to the Governor's Annual Frog Jumping Contest in Springfield.
Florence
COLUMBIA
Wilmington
Cape Fear
IT AIN'T THE SHOES!
Michael Jordan was born in Wilmington in 1963.
Myrtle Beach
The longest sand sculpture ever (10 miles long) was built in 1990 on Myrtle Beach.
SOUTH CAROLINA
Springfield
L. Marion
L. Moultrie
Augusta
Savannah
Charleston
SNAKE EYES
South Carolina has 43 kinds of snakes. GROSS!!! Look closely to see how many of these slimy snakes are slipping around in this picture.
I AM ONE SMART COOKIE!
Savannah
Stumble around at the Okefenokee Swamp, "Land of the Trembling Earth."
Georgia's nickname is "The Peach State."
CUMBERLAND I. NAT. SEASHORE
Girl Scouts, originally called the Girl Guides, was founded in Savannah in 1912.
The WRIGHT FLIGHTS
If Wilbur and Orville Wright wanted to fly their plane from Kitty Hawk to these North Carolina cities, approximately how far would each flight be? Eyeball the distance on the map and place the three following numbers in the right space: 330, 290, 200.
Kitty Hawk to Raleigh = ______ miles
Kitty Hawk to Charlotte = ______ miles
Kitty Hawk to Winston Salem = ______ miles
A B C D E F G H I J K L M N O
10 11 12 13 14 15 16 17 18 19

Florida
The biggest pizza ever made was in Tallahassee. It fed 30,000 people!
10
343
Pensacola
GULF IS. NATIONAL SEASHORE
TALLAHASSEE
F
River
Niceville
Feel lucky? Then go gator-wrestlin' at the Boggy Bayou Mullet Festival in Niceville.
Gulf of
Salty water, but...
It has Mickey.
It has sunshine.
And the Astronauts think it's a real BLAST! It's FLORIDA.
Orange ya glad it's part of the U.S.A.?
Blue Angels flight squadron is based at Pensacola Naval Air Station.
NOW, IF I COULD JUST FIND MY TOOTHBRUSH
Sponge diving is big business in the Gulf of Mexico. Especially in Tarpon Springs.
FLOWER POWER
To find Florida's state flower, take U.S. 1 to I-95 and go north to Jacksonville.
You'll see circled orange letters and the answer will blossom before your eyes!
GATOR BRIGADE
Florida is home to thousands of alligators. Can you make it from Miami to Tallahassee without getting gobbled? Let your fingers do the walking on the map as you find a safe highway route.
TRICKY TREES
Florida's state tree is the sabal palm tree. Two of the trees in this palm tree patch are identical. Can you spot them?
LAUGHABLE LAWS
Once, Floridians were required to wear clothes while taking a bath. Maybe that's why we all take a bathing suit to this sunny state!
10
1
2
3
4
5
6
7
8
9

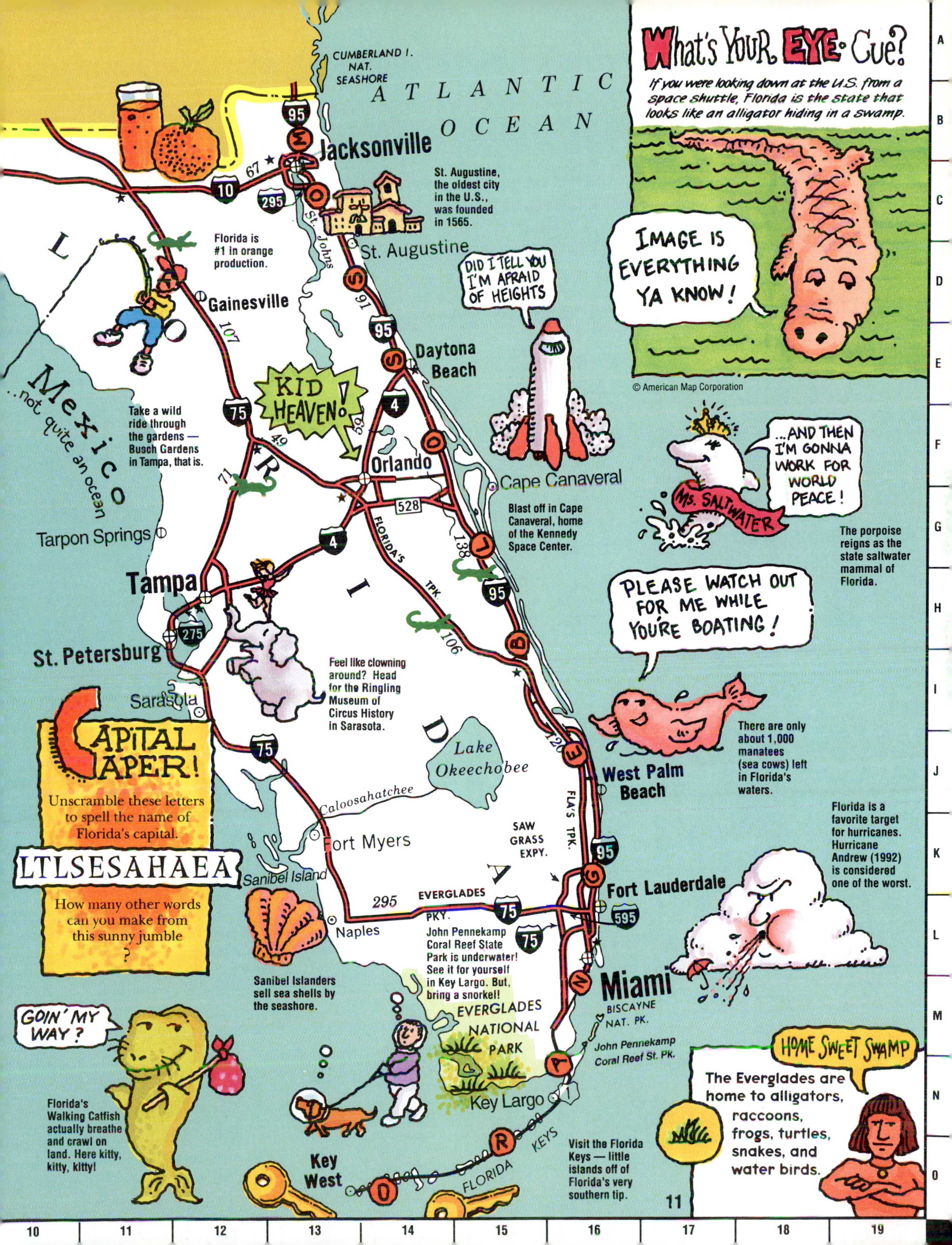

What's Your EYE-Cue?
If you were looking down at the U.S. from a space shuttle, Florida is the state that looks like an alligator hiding in a swamp.
IMAGE IS EVERYTHING YA KNOW!
© American Map Corporation
CUMBERLAND I. NAT. SEASHORE
ATLANTIC OCEAN
Jacksonville
St. Augustine, the oldest city in the U.S., was founded in 1565.
St. Augustine
St. Johns
Florida is #1 in orange production.
Gainesville
DID I TELL YOU I'M AFRAID OF HEIGHTS
Daytona Beach
KID HEAVEN!
Mexico ...not quite an ocean
Take a wild ride through the gardens — Busch Gardens in Tampa, that is.
Orlando
Cape Canaveral
Blast off in Cape Canaveral, home of the Kennedy Space Center.
...AND THEN I'M GONNA WORK FOR WORLD PEACE!
Ms. SALTWATER
The porpoise reigns as the state saltwater mammal of Florida.
Tarpon Springs
Tampa
FLORIDA'S TPK.
PLEASE WATCH OUT FOR ME WHILE YOU'RE BOATING!
St. Petersburg
Feel like clowning around? Head for the Ringling Museum of Circus History in Sarasota.
Sarasota
There are only about 1,000 manatees (sea cows) left in Florida's waters.
CAPITAL CAPER!
Unscramble these letters to spell the name of Florida's capital.
LTLSESAHAEA
How many other words can you make from this sunny jumble?
Lake Okeechobee
Caloosahatchee
West Palm Beach
FLA'S TPK.
Florida is a favorite target for hurricanes. Hurricane Andrew (1992) is considered one of the worst.
Fort Myers
SAW GRASS EXPY.
Sanibel Island
Fort Lauderdale
EVERGLADES PKY.
Naples
John Pennekamp Coral Reef State Park is underwater! See it for yourself in Key Largo. But, bring a snorkel!
Sanibel Islanders sell sea shells by the seashore.
Miami
BISCAYNE NAT. PK.
GOIN' MY WAY?
EVERGLADES NATIONAL PARK
John Pennekamp Coral Reef St. Pk.
HOME SWEET SWAMP
The Everglades are home to alligators, raccoons, frogs, turtles, snakes, and water birds.
Key Largo
Florida's Walking Catfish actually breathe and crawl on land. Here kitty, kitty, kitty!
FLORIDA KEYS
Key West
Visit the Florida Keys — little islands off of Florida's very southern tip.

NORTH CENTRAL
Dive into the lakes of the North Central States — some are small and some are GREAT!
CANADA
UNITED STATES
Lake of the Woods
Rainy Lake
Fort Frances
International Falls
VOYAGEURS NAT. PK.
Lac la Croix
Pigeon
GRAND PORTAGE
Minnesota is home of the oldest rock. It's 3.8 billion years old.
LET'S ROCK!
THERE'S NO PLACE LIKE H.O.M.E.S.
How to remember the Great Lakes: Huron, Ontario, Michigan, Erie, Superior — H.O.M.E.S.
Collect your allowance and hit The Mall of America — the world's largest shopping mall — just outside Minneapolis.
Land O' Lakes
Winnibigoshish
Source of Mississippi R.
Leech L.
Minnesota has 22,000 lakes. Over 4,000 square miles are covered by water.
In-line skates were invented by Minnesota's Scott Olson, a former pro hockey player.
Mississippi
Duluth
Superior
Ashland
APOSTLE IS. NAT. LAKESHORE
Lake
I'M ON A ROLL!
Hayward
St. Croix
ST. CROIX NAT. SCENIC RIVERWAY
MINNESOTA
Rhinelander
Skip on over to the annual Jump Rope Contest in Bloomer.
Bloomer
Eau Claire
Minneapolis
ST. PAUL
Indian peace pipes are carved from red stone found near Pipestone.
Minnesota
Lake City
WISCONSIN
Pipestone
Rochester
La Crosse
Baraboo
Wisconsin
MAD
Water skiing began on Lake Pepin in Lake City in 1922.
Don't miss the Wisconsin Dells (no matter how much your parents don't want to go).
Mississippi
BEAVER BLAST!
You're in Minneapolis, but you'd much rather be in Beaver Island, Michigan. How can you get there? It's easy! Just follow the beaver trail. Let these little guys show you the way.
LAUGHABLE LAWS
In Michigan, it was illegal to hitch a crocodile to a fire hydrant. (Don't ask what crocodiles were doing in Michigan in the first place!)
MAP MANIA!
It's time to play CAPITAL COORDINATES! Locate these state capitals and then write in their map coordinates.
(See MAPMANIA in the Southeast region to learn how to read coordinates.)
St. Paul, Minnesota
Lansing, Michigan
Madison, Wisconsin
Letter(s)
Number
Wisconsin dairy cows produce enough milk to fill an olympic-size pool 11 times a day!
1 2 3 4 5 6 7 8 9

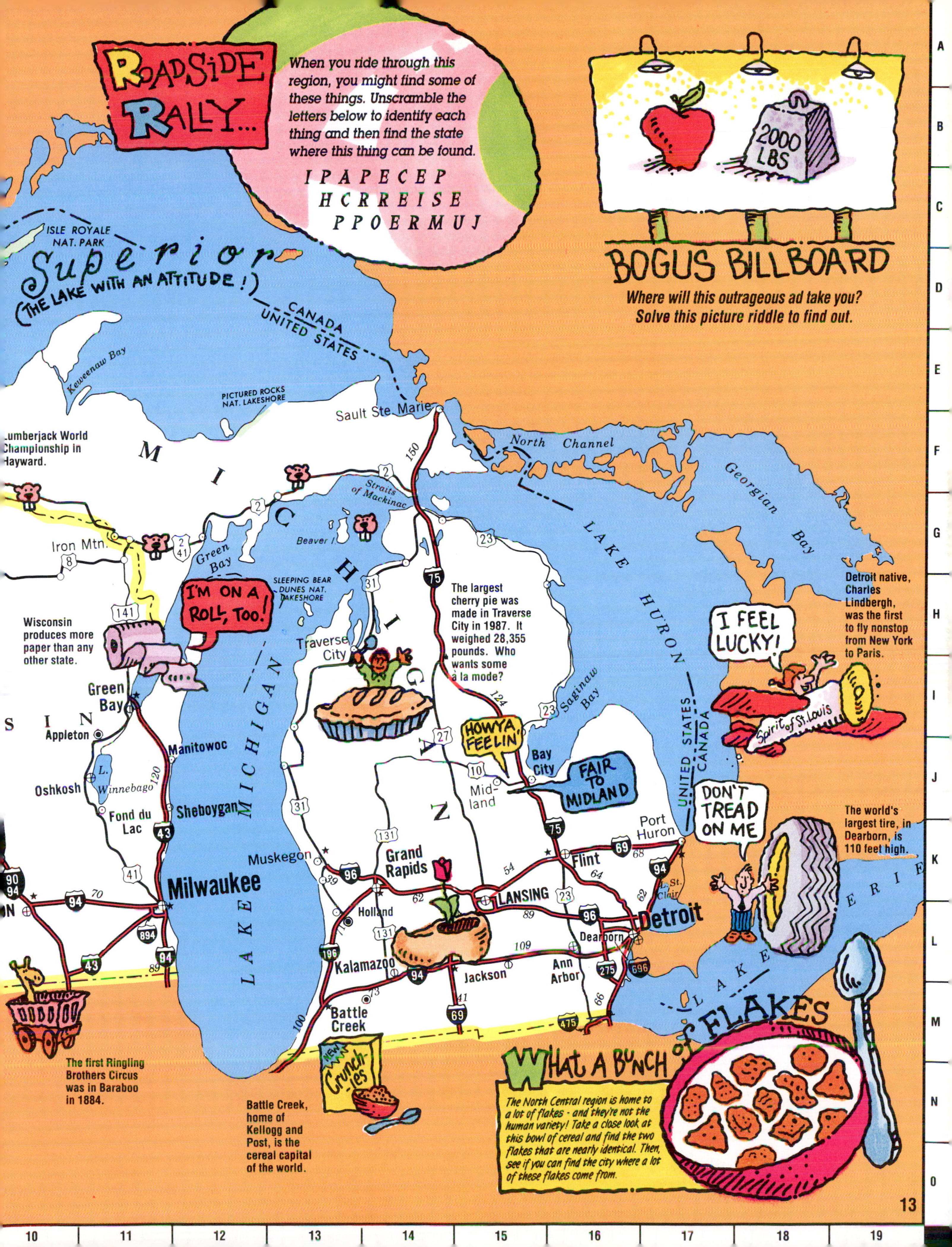
ROADSIDE RALLY...
When you ride through this region, you might find some of these things. Unscramble the letters below to identify each thing and then find the state where this thing can be found.
IPAPECEP
HCRREISE
PPOERMUJ
BOGUS BILLBOARD
Where will this outrageous ad take you? Solve this picture riddle to find out.
2000 LBS
Superior (THE LAKE WITH AN ATTITUDE!)
ISLE ROYALE NAT. PARK
CANADA
UNITED STATES
Keweenaw Bay
PICTURED ROCKS NAT. LAKESHORE
Sault Ste. Marie
North Channel
Georgian Bay
Straits of Mackinac
Beaver I.
MICHIGAN
LAKE HURON
LAKE MICHIGAN
Lumberjack World Championship in Hayward.
Iron Mtn.
Green Bay
SLEEPING BEAR DUNES NAT. LAKESHORE
I'M ON A ROLL, TOO!
Wisconsin produces more paper than any other state.
Traverse City
The largest cherry pie was made in Traverse City in 1987. It weighed 28,355 pounds. Who wants some à la mode?
Detroit native, Charles Lindbergh, was the first to fly nonstop from New York to Paris.
I FEEL LUCKY!
Spirit of St. Louis
Saginaw Bay
HOWYA FEELIN'
Bay City
FAIR TO MIDLAND
Midland
Green Bay
Appleton
Oshkosh
L. Winnebago
Manitowoc
Fond du Lac
Sheboygan
Milwaukee
DON'T TREAD ON ME
The world's largest tire, in Dearborn, is 110 feet high.
Port Huron
Muskegon
Grand Rapids
Flint
LANSING
Holland
Detroit
L. St. Clair
Dearborn
Kalamazoo
Jackson
Ann Arbor
Battle Creek
LAKE ERIE
The first Ringling Brothers Circus was in Baraboo in 1884.
NEW Crunchies
Battle Creek, home of Kellogg and Post, is the cereal capital of the world.
WHAT A BUNCH OF FLAKES
The North Central region is home to a lot of flakes - and they're not the human variety! Take a close look at this bowl of cereal and find the two flakes that are nearly identical. Then, see if you can find the city where a lot of these flakes come from.

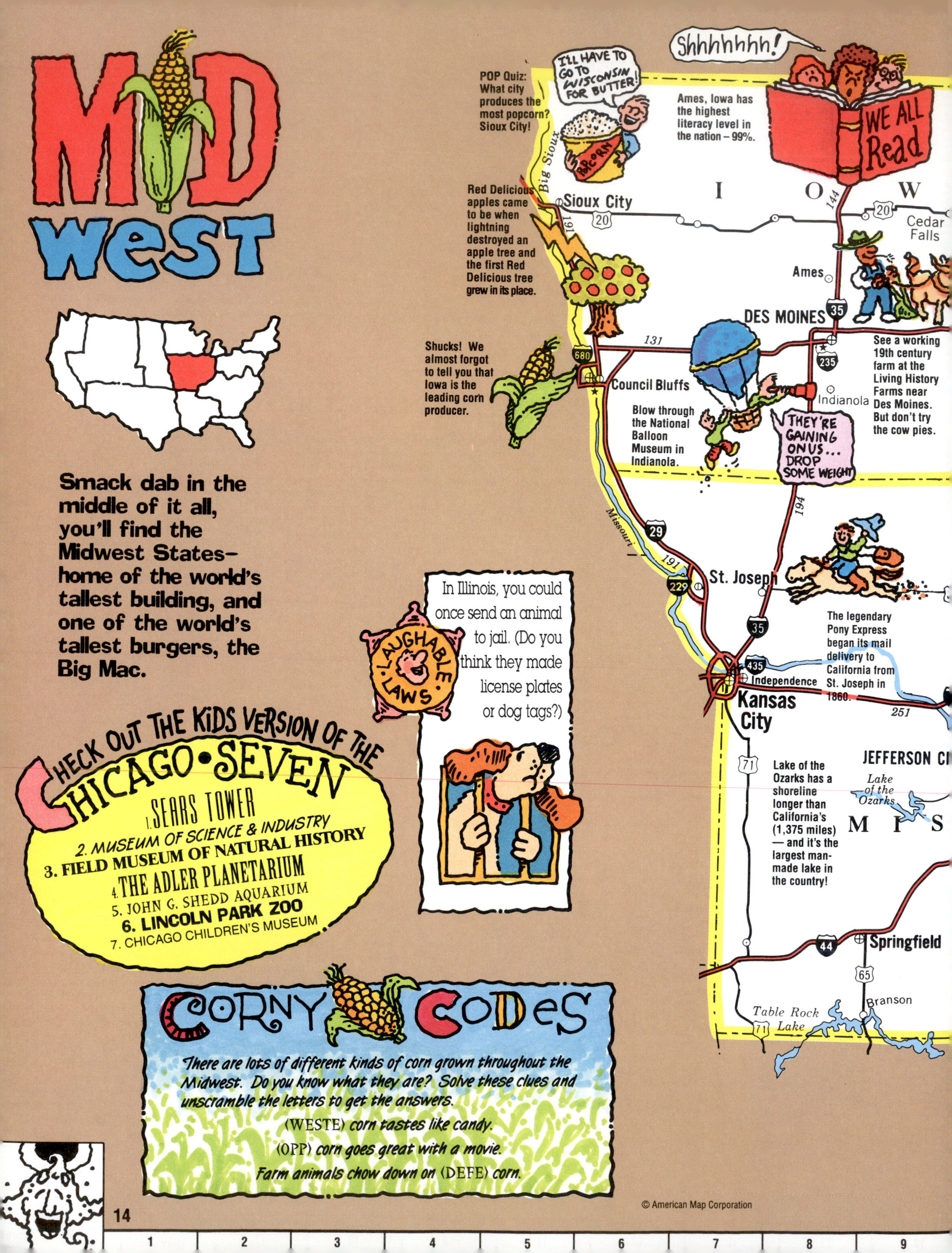
MID west
Smack dab in the middle of it all, you'll find the Midwest States–home of the world's tallest building, and one of the world's tallest burgers, the Big Mac.
CHECK OUT THE KIDS VERSION OF THE CHICAGO • SEVEN
1. SEARS TOWER
2. MUSEUM OF SCIENCE & INDUSTRY
3. FIELD MUSEUM OF NATURAL HISTORY
4. THE ADLER PLANETARIUM
5. JOHN G. SHEDD AQUARIUM
6. LINCOLN PARK ZOO
7. CHICAGO CHILDREN'S MUSEUM
LAUGHABLE LAWS
In Illinois, you could once send an animal to jail. (Do you think they made license plates or dog tags?)
CORNY CODES
There are lots of different kinds of corn grown throughout the Midwest. Do you know what they are? Solve these clues and unscramble the letters to get the answers.
(WESTE) corn tastes like candy.
(OPP) corn goes great with a movie.
Farm animals chow down on (DEFE) corn.
POP Quiz: What city produces the most popcorn? Sioux City!
I'LL HAVE TO GO TO WISCONSIN FOR BUTTER!
POPCORN
Shhhhhhh!
Ames, Iowa has the highest literacy level in the nation – 99%.
WE ALL Read
Red Delicious apples came to be when lightning destroyed an apple tree and the first Red Delicious tree grew in its place.
Shucks! We almost forgot to tell you that Iowa is the leading corn producer.
Blow through the National Balloon Museum in Indianola.
THEY'RE GAINING ON US... DROP SOME WEIGHT!
See a working 19th century farm at the Living History Farms near Des Moines. But don't try the cow pies.
The legendary Pony Express began its mail delivery to California from St. Joseph in 1860.
Lake of the Ozarks has a shoreline longer than California's (1,375 miles) — and it's the largest man-made lake in the country!
I O W
M I S
Big Sioux
Sioux City
Cedar Falls
Ames
DES MOINES
Council Bluffs
Indianola
Missouri
St. Joseph
Independence
Kansas City
JEFFERSON CI
Lake of the Ozarks
Springfield
Branson
Table Rock Lake
20
191
144
35
131
680
235
29
194
229
435
251
71
44
65
© American Map Corporation
1 2 3 4 5 6 7 8 9

RACE TO INDY
On your mark, get set, and find TWO cities that are approximately 250 miles away from Indianapolis, home of the Indy 500. Make a straight line using the unit of measure below.
50 miles x 5 = 250
50 MILES
Dubuque is home of the steepest and shortest railroad. It has a 60 degree incline and is 296 feet long.
The Sears Tower is the tallest building in the world. Wouldn't it be cool to spit off the top?
LAKE MICHIGAN
Planely speaking, O'Hare International Airport is the world's busiest.
Waterloo
Dubuque
Cedar Rapids
Iowa City
Davenport
Moline
Rockford
Elgin
Des Plaines
Chicago
Aurora
Joliet
Gary
South Bend
Elkhart
IND. E. W. TOLL RD.
Fort Wayne
Amish communities near Berne use little or no modern technology. (That means no video games.)
Ray Kroc opened the first McDonald's in Des Plaines in 1955. Let's all give McThanks!
Visit Waterslide Park in Davenport near I-80.
Take a spin around the two Six Flags amusement parks — one near Chicago and one in St. Louis!
Peoria
Kokomo
Berne
Lafayette
INDIANA
Anderson
The Tom Sawyer Fence Painting Contest is in Hannibal, home of Mark Twain.
READY, SET, GO to Indianapolis, home of the Indy 500.
Champaign
Richmond
INDIANAPOLIS
Hannibal
SPRINGFIELD
Decatur
Shelbyville
Terre Haute
Missouri was named by Indians and means "muddy water."
ILLINOIS
Martinsville
Larry Bird was born in French Lick.
YOUR NAME IS MUD!
AT LEAST I WAS BORN HERE
French Lick
St. Louis
Missouri
Meramac Caves
Louisville
Evansville
It's called "The Land of Lincoln," but Ronald Reagan was the only president born in Illinois.
HOW MUCH LONGER DAD?
Gateway Arch in St. Louis marks the spot where thousands crossed the Mississippi heading west.
OZARK NAT. SCENIC RIVERWAYS
WHO'S YOUR HOOSIER?
What's with all these towns named after nerdy guys? Who is Martin and why did they name Martinsville after him? Find more of these Hoosier-villes by following the coordinates listed below.
K-15
E-18
H-17
DONT LOOK AT ME... I'M HIDING
Missouri has more caves than any other state, including Meramec Cave — the hideout of outlaw Jesse James.
MAP Mania
Times are a changin', especially in the Midwest. There are two different time zones in this region: Eastern time and Central time. The dividing line runs along the Illinois/Indiana border. So, when it's 1:00 p.m. in Chicago, it's 2:00 p.m. (one hour later) in Indiana. Test your time zone knowledge with this timely story problem: You leave Springfield, Illinois at 10:00 a.m. and drive to Indianapolis, Indiana. The drive takes five hours. What time is it when you arrive?

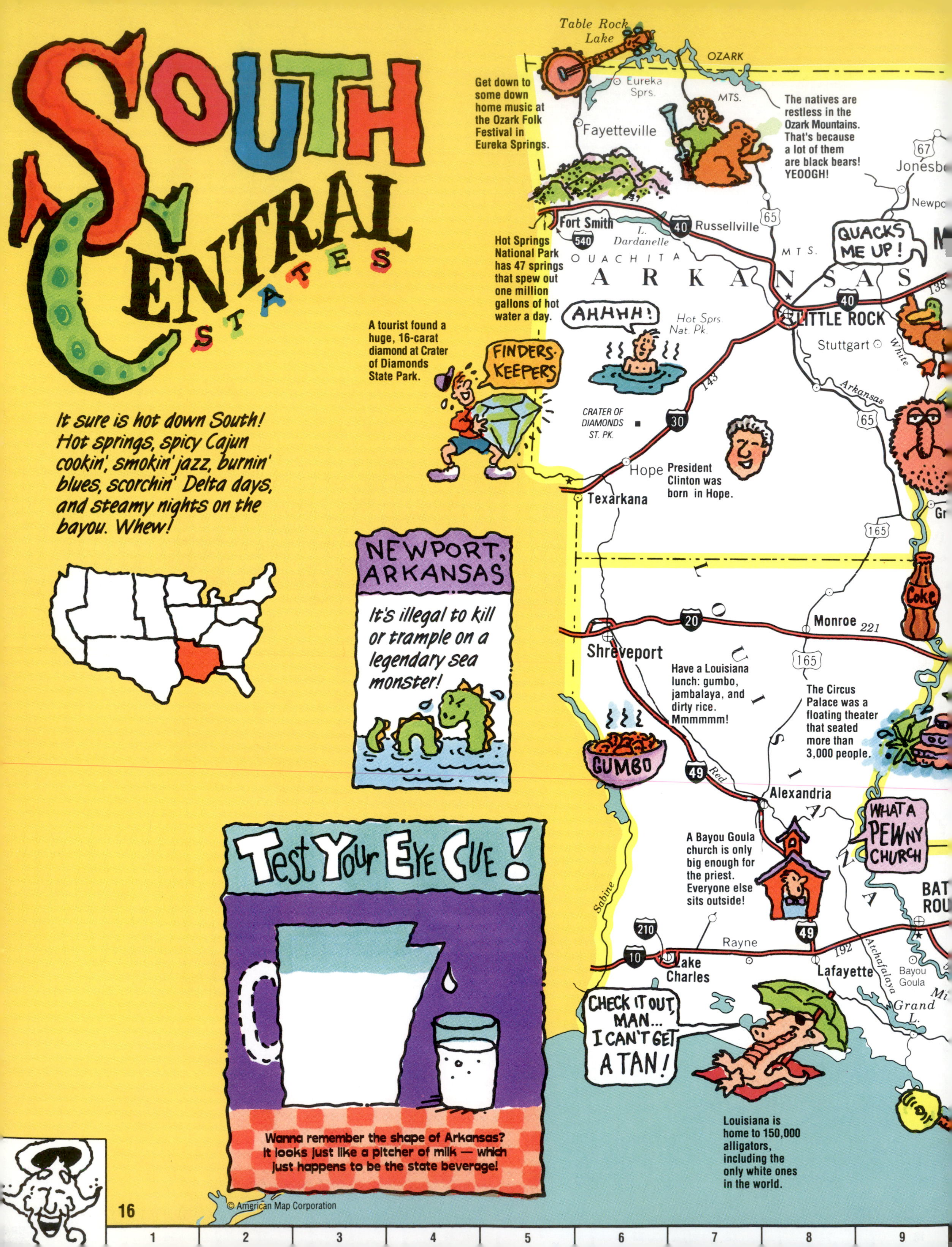

SOUTH CENTRAL STATES
It sure is hot down South! Hot springs, spicy Cajun cookin', smokin' jazz, burnin' blues, scorchin' Delta days, and steamy nights on the bayou. Whew!
Table Rock Lake
OZARK
MTS.
Eureka Sprs.
Get down to some down home music at the Ozark Folk Festival in Eureka Springs.
Fayetteville
The natives are restless in the Ozark Mountains. That's because a lot of them are black bears! YEOOGH!
67
Jonesb
Newp
Fort Smith
540
L. Dardanelle
40
Russellville
65
OUACHITA
MTS.
QUACKS ME UP!
ARKANSAS
Hot Springs National Park has 47 springs that spew out one million gallons of hot water a day.
AHHHH!
Hot Sprs. Nat. Pk.
40
LITTLE ROCK
Stuttgart
White
Arkansas
138
65
A tourist found a huge, 16-carat diamond at Crater of Diamonds State Park.
FINDERS KEEPERS
CRATER OF DIAMONDS ST. PK.
143
30
Hope
President Clinton was born in Hope.
Texarkana
165
NEWPORT, ARKANSAS
It's illegal to kill or trample on a legendary sea monster!
Coke
LOUISIANA
20
Monroe
221
Shreveport
165
Have a Louisiana lunch: gumbo, jambalaya, and dirty rice. Mmmmmm!
The Circus Palace was a floating theater that seated more than 3,000 people.
GUMBO
49
Red
Alexandria
WHAT A PEWNY CHURCH
A Bayou Goula church is only big enough for the priest. Everyone else sits outside!
Test Your Eye Cue!
Sabine
BAT ROU
210
49
Rayne
10
Lake Charles
192
Lafayette
Atchafalaya
Bayou Goula
Grand L.
CHECK IT OUT, MAN... I CAN'T GET A TAN!
Wanna remember the shape of Arkansas? It looks just like a pitcher of milk — which just happens to be the state beverage!
Louisiana is home to 150,000 alligators, including the only white ones in the world.
© American Map Corporation
1 2 3 4 5 6 7 8 9

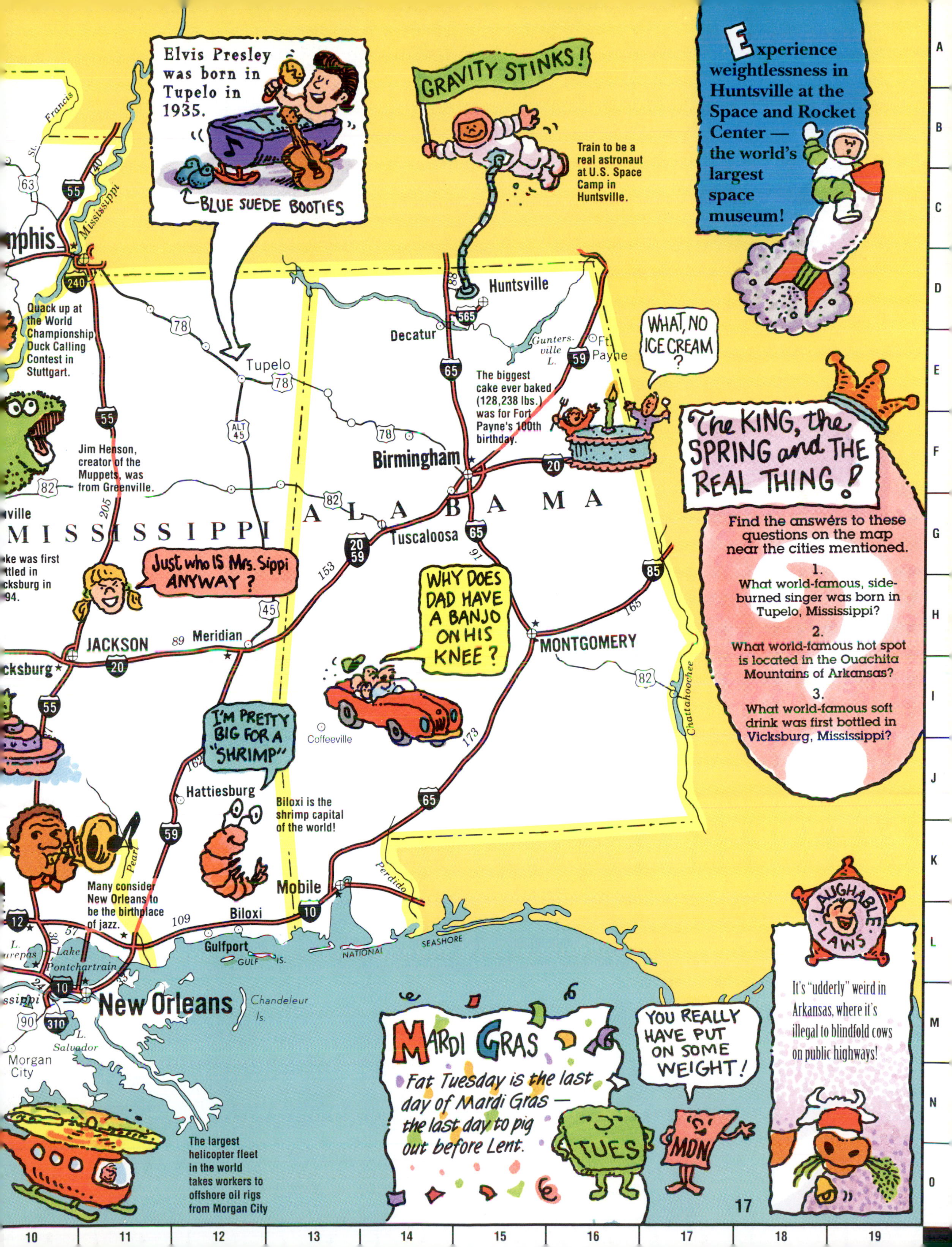

Elvis Presley was born in Tupelo in 1935.
BLUE SUEDE BOOTIES
GRAVITY STINKS!
Train to be a real astronaut at U.S. Space Camp in Huntsville.
Experience weightlessness in Huntsville at the Space and Rocket Center — the world's largest space museum!
Quack up at the World Championship Duck Calling Contest in Stuttgart.
WHAT, NO ICE CREAM?
The biggest cake ever baked (128,238 lbs.) was for Fort Payne's 100th birthday.
Jim Henson, creator of the Muppets, was from Greenville.
The KING, the SPRING and THE REAL THING!
Find the answers to these questions on the map near the cities mentioned.
1. What world-famous, side-burned singer was born in Tupelo, Mississippi?
2. What world-famous hot spot is located in the Ouachita Mountains of Arkansas?
3. What world-famous soft drink was first bottled in Vicksburg, Mississippi?
Just who IS Mrs. Sippi ANYWAY?
WHY DOES DAD HAVE A BANJO ON HIS KNEE?
I'M PRETTY BIG FOR A "SHRIMP"
Biloxi is the shrimp capital of the world!
Many consider New Orleans to be the birthplace of jazz.
LAUGHABLE LAWS
It's "udderly" weird in Arkansas, where it's illegal to blindfold cows on public highways!
MARDI GRAS
Fat Tuesday is the last day of Mardi Gras — the last day to pig out before Lent.
YOU REALLY HAVE PUT ON SOME WEIGHT!
TUES
MON
The largest helicopter fleet in the world takes workers to offshore oil rigs from Morgan City
MISSISSIPPI
ALABAMA
Memphis
Huntsville
Decatur
Guntersville L.
Ft. Payne
Tupelo
Birmingham
Tuscaloosa
JACKSON
Meridian
Vicksburg
MONTGOMERY
Coffeeville
Hattiesburg
Mobile
Biloxi
Gulfport
GULF IS. NATIONAL SEASHORE
New Orleans
Lake Pontchartrain
Chandeleur Is.
L. Salvador
Morgan City
Mississippi
St. Francis
Chattahoochee
Perdido
Pearl

The Plains States were once the wild frontier—home of famous cowboys and Indians, traders, explorers, railroads, and The Pony Express. No wonder they call 'em great!

PLAINS STATES

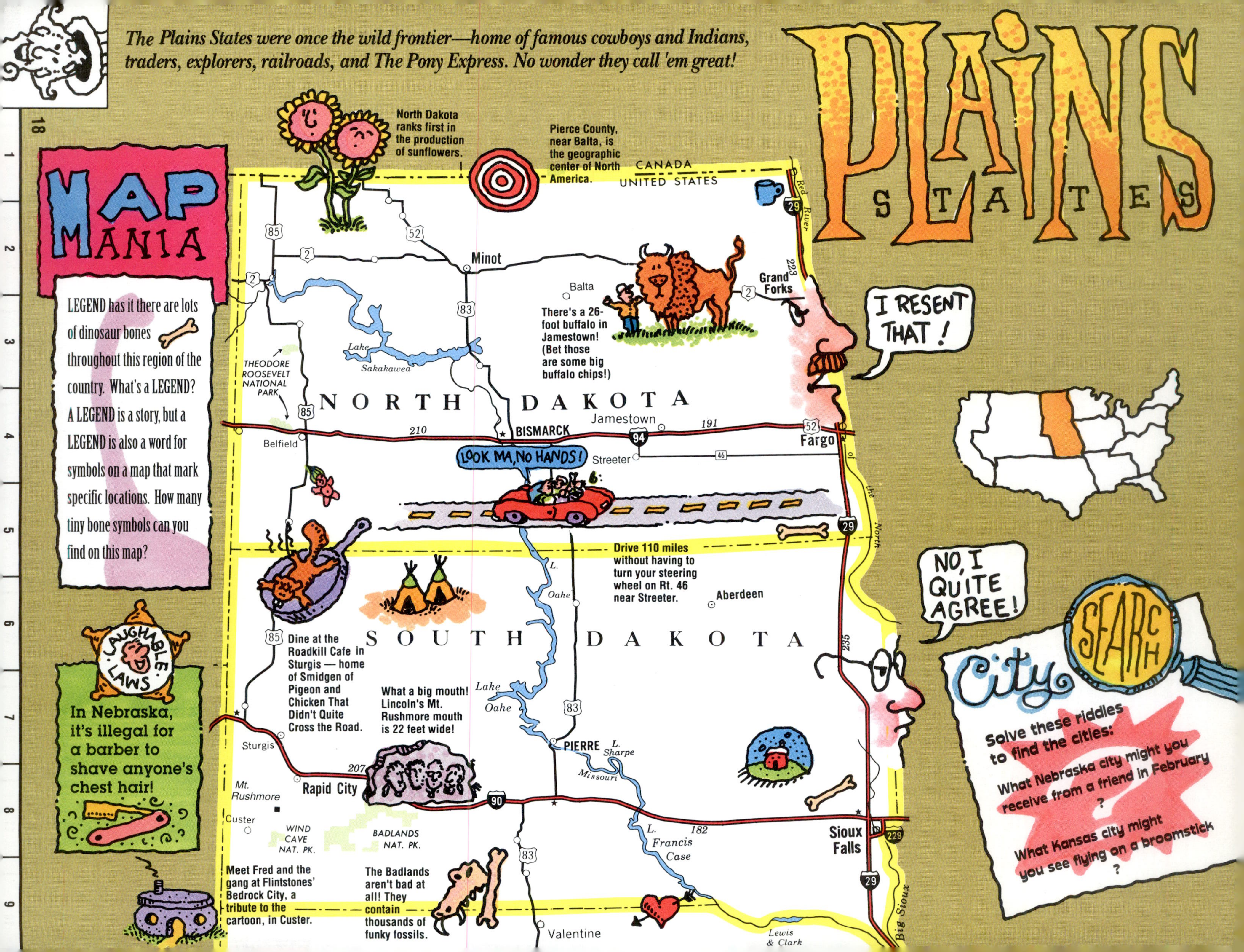

NEBRASKA
KANSAS
Nebraska's nickname was "The Bug Eating State" before it was changed to "The Cornhusker State."
WHAT'S WRONG WITH EATING BUGS?
Scottsbluff
The world's first rodeo was held in North Platte in 1882 and starred Buffalo Bill.
North Platte
The world's first and only roller skating museum is in Lincoln.
FACE IT, WE ARE BORING!
Every year, Seward residents invite a family traveling along the highway to lead their 4th of July parade.
Omaha
Seward
LINCOLN
HOMESTEAD
Missouri
I DON'T FEEL SO LUCKY...
Amelia Earhart, the first woman to fly solo across the Atlantic, was born in Atchison.
Atchison
Kansas City
Kansas City
Lebanon is the belly button of the nation — it's the exact center of the U.S.A.
Lebanon
I THINK I'M AN "INNIE"
TOPEKA
KANSAS TURNPIKE
Salina
Dodge City
Arkansas
Wichita
Liberal
Swallow a stack of flapjacks at the International Pancake Race in Liberal.
OH, TOTO... NOT AGAIN!
Kansas has more tornadoes than any other state!
SPEAK FOR YOUR-SELF BREAD HEAD
TORNADO TWISTER
Hold on to your hats in the Plains States because there are lots of tornadoes in this region. Can you make it from Wichita to Omaha without getting blown away? You'll see mini-tornadoes in the road. When you come across one, choose another route. There's only one path that will get you there safely.
ROADKILL SCRAMBLE
Here's a good 'n gross game if you have the guts to play it! Unscramble the names of these frequently found flattened friends.
KSUNK
SPMOUS
OCRONAC
Prooooey
REST STOP ROUND-UP
Rest-stop gift shops have some pretty tacky junk — postcards, mugs, troll dolls, baseball caps, and those funny snow globes filled with weird stuff. Each of these items are hidden on this map. Find all five and you're king of the road!
© American Map Corporation

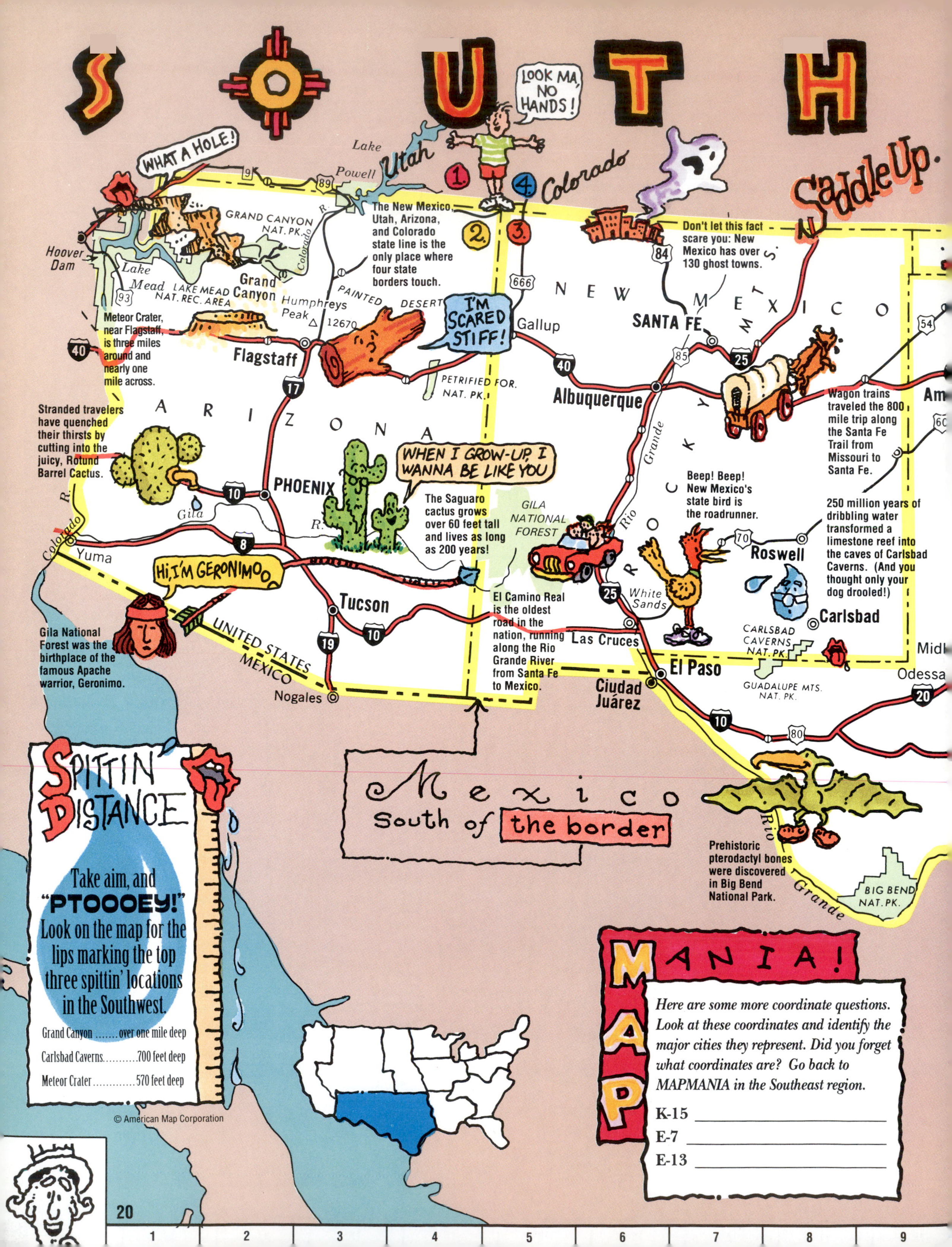
SOUTH
LOOK MA, NO HANDS!
Saddle Up.
WHAT A HOLE!
Lake Powell
Utah
Colorado
1
2
3
4
The New Mexico, Utah, Arizona, and Colorado state line is the only place where four state borders touch.
Don't let this fact scare you: New Mexico has over 130 ghost towns.
GRAND CANYON NAT. PK.
Hoover Dam
Lake Mead
LAKE MEAD NAT. REC. AREA
Grand Canyon
Humphreys Peak 12670
PAINTED DESERT
I'M SCARED STIFF!
Gallup
NEW MEXICO
SANTA FE
Meteor Crater, near Flagstaff, is three miles around and nearly one mile across.
Flagstaff
PETRIFIED FOR. NAT. PK.
Albuquerque
Stranded travelers have quenched their thirsts by cutting into the juicy, Rotund Barrel Cactus.
ARIZONA
Wagon trains traveled the 800 mile trip along the Santa Fe Trail from Missouri to Santa Fe.
WHEN I GROW-UP, I WANNA BE LIKE YOU
ROCKY MTS.
Rio Grande
Beep! Beep! New Mexico's state bird is the roadrunner.
PHOENIX
Gila R.
The Saguaro cactus grows over 60 feet tall and lives as long as 200 years!
GILA NATIONAL FOREST
250 million years of dribbling water transformed a limestone reef into the caves of Carlsbad Caverns. (And you thought only your dog drooled!)
Roswell
Colorado R.
Yuma
HI, I'M GERONIMO
Tucson
White Sands
El Camino Real is the oldest road in the nation, running along the Rio Grande River from Santa Fe to Mexico.
Las Cruces
CARLSBAD CAVERNS NAT. PK.
Carlsbad
UNITED STATES
MEXICO
Gila National Forest was the birthplace of the famous Apache warrior, Geronimo.
Nogales
Ciudad Juárez
El Paso
GUADALUPE MTS. NAT. PK.
Odessa
SPITTIN' DISTANCE
Take aim, and "PTOOOEY!" Look on the map for the lips marking the top three spittin' locations in the Southwest.
Grand Canyon .... over one mile deep
Carlsbad Caverns .... 700 feet deep
Meteor Crater .... 570 feet deep
Mexico
South of the border
Prehistoric pterodactyl bones were discovered in Big Bend National Park.
Rio Grande
BIG BEND NAT. PK.
MAP MANIA!
Here are some more coordinate questions. Look at these coordinates and identify the major cities they represent. Did you forget what coordinates are? Go back to MAPMANIA in the Southeast region.
K-15 ____________
E-7 ____________
E-13 ____________
© American Map Corporation
20
1 2 3 4 5 6 7 8 9

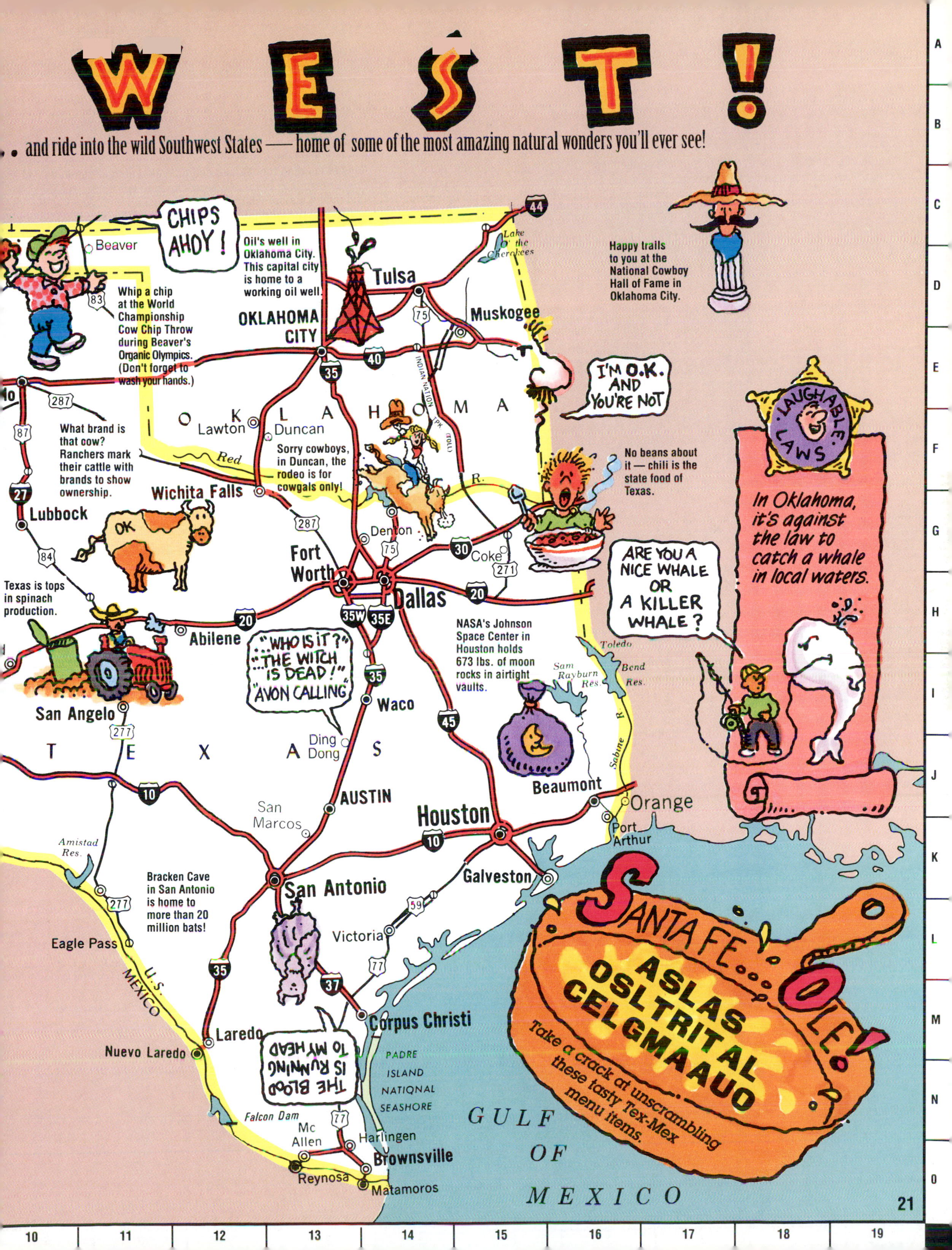

WEST!
. . and ride into the wild Southwest States — home of some of the most amazing natural wonders you'll ever see!
CHIPS AHOY!
Beaver
Whip a chip at the World Championship Cow Chip Throw during Beaver's Organic Olympics. (Don't forget to wash your hands.)
Oil's well in Oklahoma City. This capital city is home to a working oil well.
Tulsa
OKLAHOMA CITY
Muskogee
Lake o' the Cherokees
Happy trails to you at the National Cowboy Hall of Fame in Oklahoma City.
I'M O.K. AND YOU'RE NOT
OKLAHOMA
Lawton
Duncan
Red R.
INDIAN NATION TPK (TOLL)
What brand is that cow? Ranchers mark their cattle with brands to show ownership.
Sorry cowboys, in Duncan, the rodeo is for cowgals only!
No beans about it — chili is the state food of Texas.
LAUGHABLE LAWS
In Oklahoma, it's against the law to catch a whale in local waters.
Wichita Falls
Lubbock
OK
Denton
Fort Worth
Dallas
Coke
ARE YOU A NICE WHALE OR A KILLER WHALE?
Texas is tops in spinach production.
Abilene
"WHO IS IT?" "THE WITCH IS DEAD!" "AVON CALLING"
NASA's Johnson Space Center in Houston holds 673 lbs. of moon rocks in airtight vaults.
Toledo Bend Res.
Sam Rayburn Res.
Sabine R.
San Angelo
Waco
Ding Dong
TEXAS
AUSTIN
Houston
Beaumont
Orange
Port Arthur
San Marcos
Amistad Res.
Bracken Cave in San Antonio is home to more than 20 million bats!
San Antonio
Galveston
Victoria
Eagle Pass
U.S.
MEXICO
Laredo
Nuevo Laredo
Corpus Christi
THE BLOOD IS RUNNING TO MY HEAD
PADRE ISLAND NATIONAL SEASHORE
Falcon Dam
Mc Allen
Harlingen
Brownsville
Reynosa
Matamoros
GULF OF MEXICO
SANTA FE...OLE!
ASLAS
OSLTRITAL
CELGMAAUO
Take a crack at unscrambling these tasty Tex-Mex menu items.
21

The Mountain States

Take a peek at the mighty peaks of the Mountain States. The terrain is rugged, rocky, and really incredible! If you dream of climbing mountains, these states are tops!

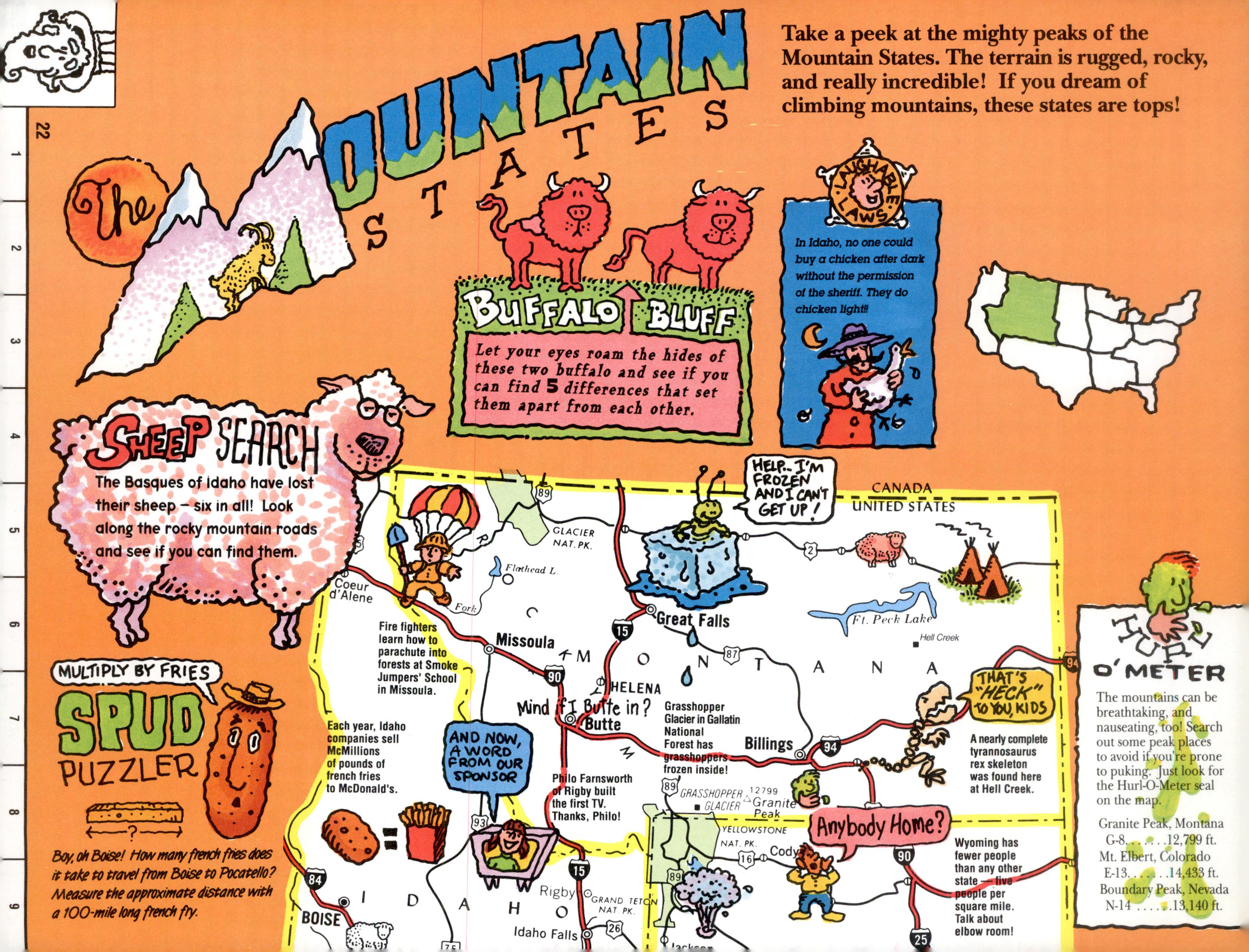

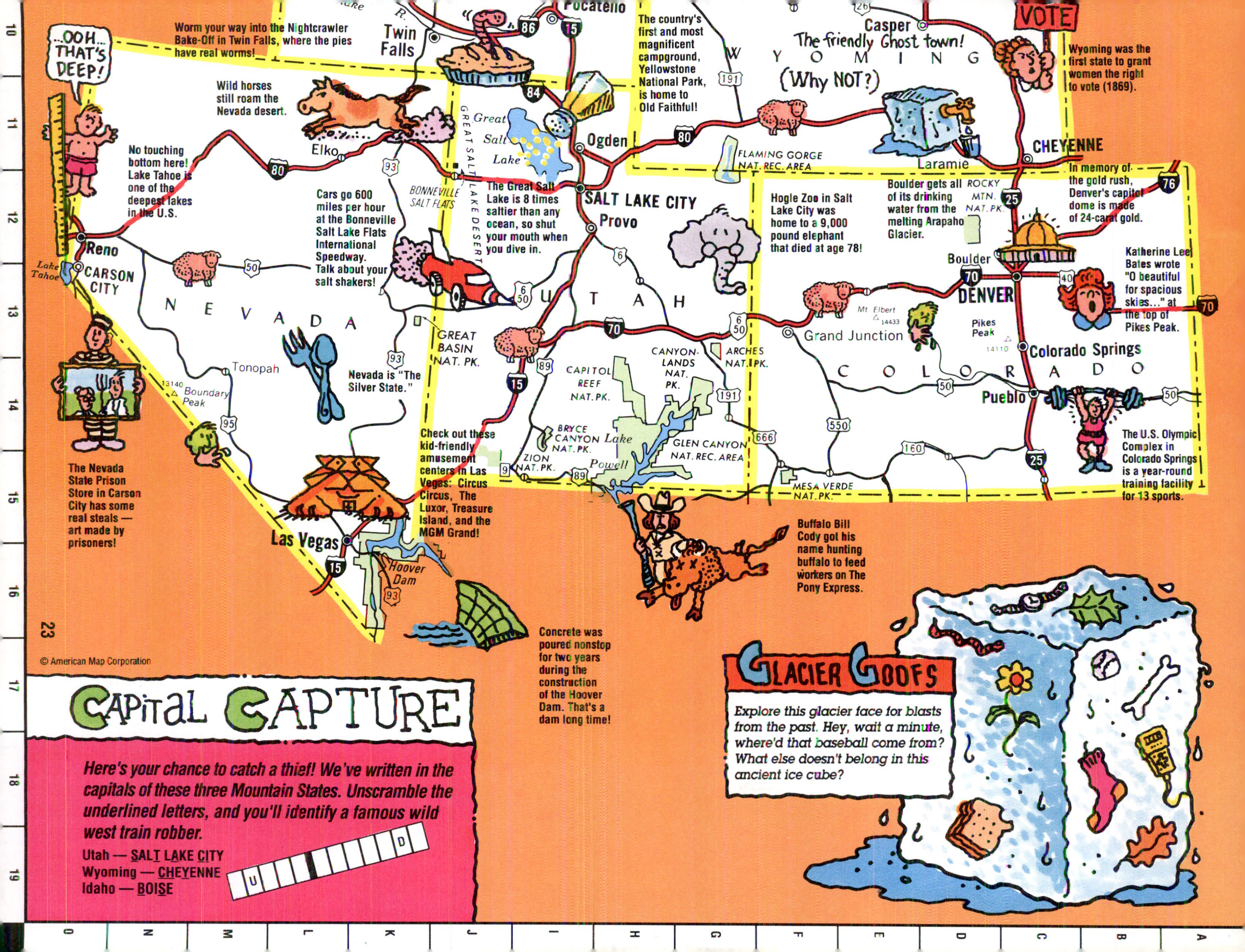

© American Map Corporation

CAPITAL CAPTURE

Here's your chance to catch a thief! We've written in the capitals of these three Mountain States. Unscramble the underlined letters, and you'll identify a famous wild west train robber.

Utah — SALT LAKE CITY
Wyoming — CHEYENNE
Idaho — BOISE

U _ _ _ _ _ _ _ _ D _

GLACIER GOOFS

Explore this glacier face for blasts from the past. Hey, wait a minute, where'd that baseball come from? What else doesn't belong in this ancient ice cube?

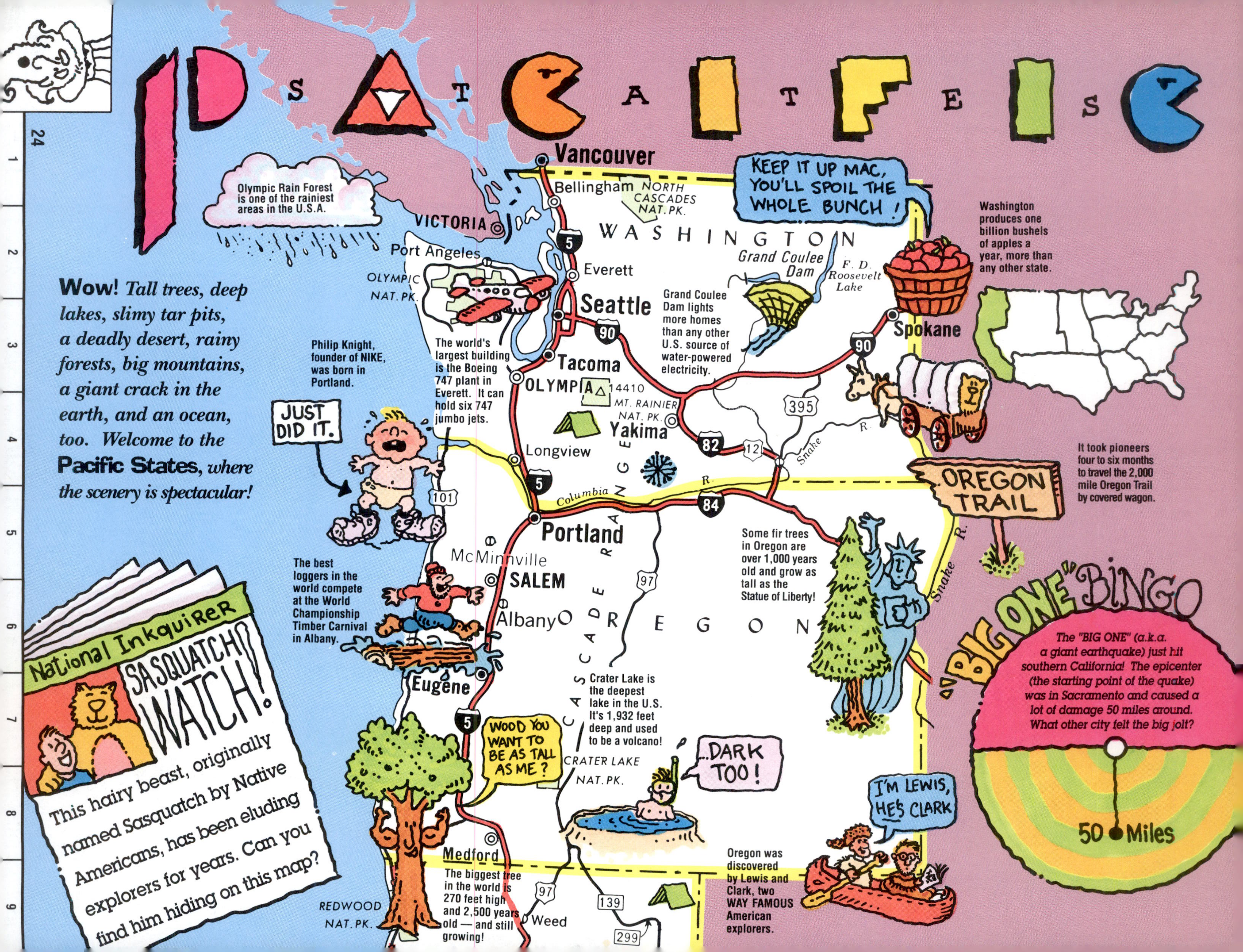

PACIFIC STATES
Wow! Tall trees, deep lakes, slimy tar pits, a deadly desert, rainy forests, big mountains, a giant crack in the earth, and an ocean, too. Welcome to the Pacific States, where the scenery is spectacular!
Olympic Rain Forest is one of the rainiest areas in the U.S.A.
Philip Knight, founder of NIKE, was born in Portland.
JUST DID IT.
The world's largest building is the Boeing 747 plant in Everett. It can hold six 747 jumbo jets.
KEEP IT UP MAC, YOU'LL SPOIL THE WHOLE BUNCH!
Washington produces one billion bushels of apples a year, more than any other state.
Grand Coulee Dam lights more homes than any other U.S. source of water-powered electricity.
It took pioneers four to six months to travel the 2,000 mile Oregon Trail by covered wagon.
OREGON TRAIL
Some fir trees in Oregon are over 1,000 years old and grow as tall as the Statue of Liberty!
The best loggers in the world compete at the World Championship Timber Carnival in Albany.
Crater Lake is the deepest lake in the U.S. It's 1,932 feet deep and used to be a volcano!
...DARK TOO!
WOOD YOU WANT TO BE AS TALL AS ME?
The biggest tree in the world is 270 feet high and 2,500 years old — and still growing!
Oregon was discovered by Lewis and Clark, two WAY FAMOUS American explorers.
I'M LEWIS, HE'S CLARK
"BIG ONE" BINGO
The "BIG ONE" (a.k.a. a giant earthquake) just hit southern California! The epicenter (the starting point of the quake) was in Sacramento and caused a lot of damage 50 miles around. What other city felt the big jolt?
50 Miles
National Inkquirer
SASQUATCH WATCH!
This hairy beast, originally named Sasquatch by Native Americans, has been eluding explorers for years. Can you find him hiding on this map?
Vancouver
VICTORIA
Bellingham
NORTH CASCADES NAT. PK.
WASHINGTON
Port Angeles
OLYMPIC NAT. PK.
Everett
Seattle
Grand Coulee Dam
F. D. Roosevelt Lake
Spokane
Tacoma
OLYMPIA
14410
MT. RAINIER NAT. PK.
Yakima
Longview
Columbia R.
Snake R.
CASCADE RANGE
Portland
McMinnville
SALEM
Albany
OREGON
Eugene
CRATER LAKE NAT. PK.
Medford
REDWOOD NAT. PK.
Weed
5
90
82
12
395
84
101
97
139
299
1
2
3
4
5
6
7
8
9

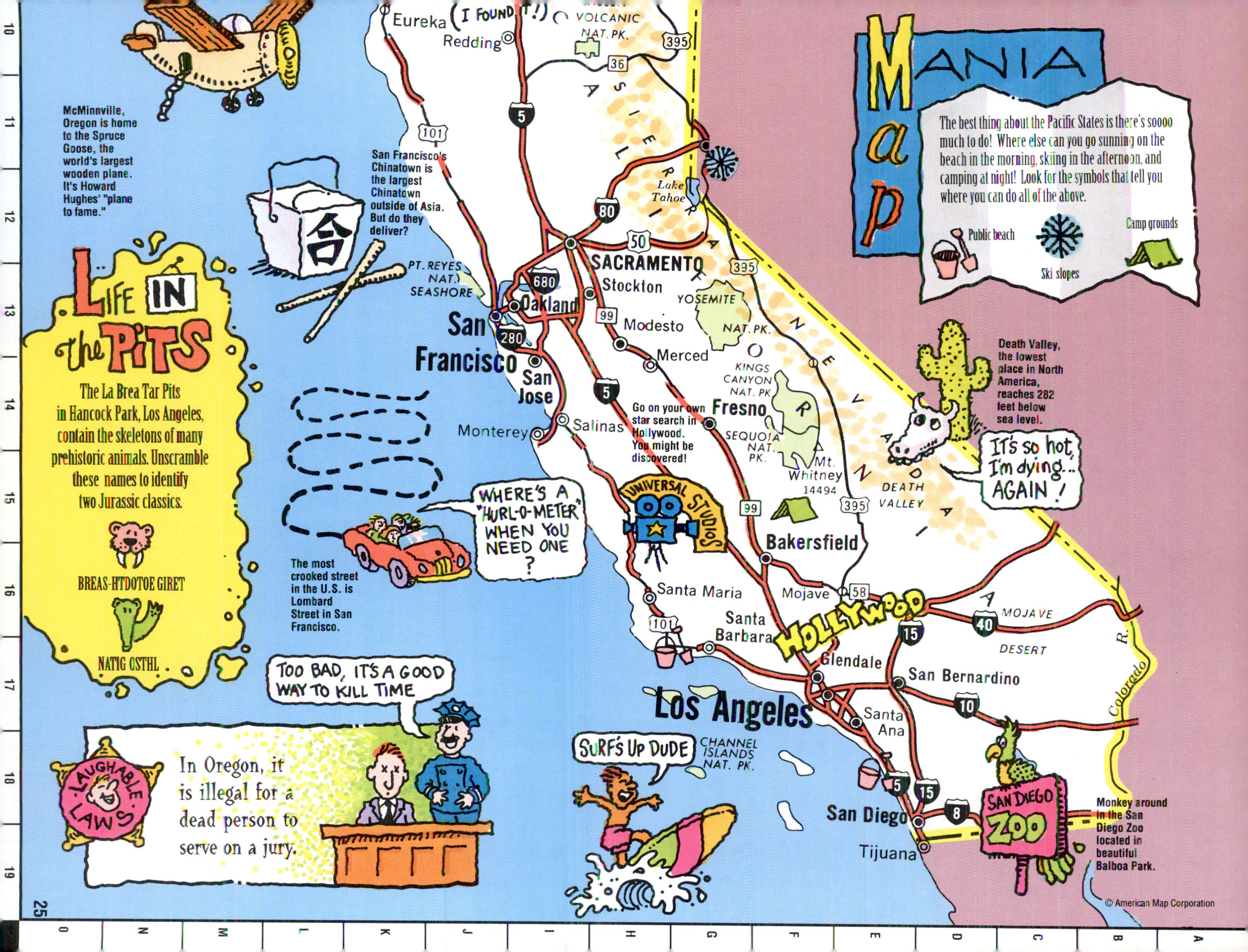

MANIA Map
The best thing about the Pacific States is there's soooo much to do! Where else can you go sunning on the beach in the morning, skiing in the afternoon, and camping at night! Look for the symbols that tell you where you can do all of the above.
Public beach
Ski slopes
Camp grounds
McMinnville, Oregon is home to the Spruce Goose, the world's largest wooden plane. It's Howard Hughes' "plane to fame."
San Francisco's Chinatown is the largest Chinatown outside of Asia. But do they deliver?
LIFE IN the PITS
The La Brea Tar Pits in Hancock Park, Los Angeles, contain the skeletons of many prehistoric animals. Unscramble these names to identify two Jurassic classics.
BREAS-HTDOTOE GIRET
NATIG OSTHL
The most crooked street in the U.S. is Lombard Street in San Francisco.
WHERE'S A "HURL-O-METER" WHEN YOU NEED ONE ?
Go on your own star search in Hollywood. You might be discovered!
Death Valley, the lowest place in North America, reaches 282 feet below sea level.
IT'S so hot, I'm dying... AGAIN!
TOO BAD, IT'S A GOOD WAY TO KILL TIME
LAUGHABLE LAWS
In Oregon, it is illegal for a dead person to serve on a jury.
SURF'S UP DUDE
Monkey around in the San Diego Zoo located in beautiful Balboa Park.
SAN DIEGO ZOO
UNIVERSAL STUDIOS
HOLLYWOOD
Eureka
(I FOUND IT!)
Redding
VOLCANIC NAT. PK.
SIERRA NEVADA
Lake Tahoe
SACRAMENTO
Stockton
Oakland
San Francisco
San Jose
PT. REYES NAT. SEASHORE
Modesto
Merced
YOSEMITE NAT. PK.
KINGS CANYON NAT. PK.
Fresno
SEQUOIA NAT. PK.
Mt. Whitney 14494
Monterey
Salinas
DEATH VALLEY
Bakersfield
Mojave
Santa Maria
Santa Barbara
Glendale
San Bernardino
MOJAVE DESERT
Colorado R.
Los Angeles
Santa Ana
CHANNEL ISLANDS NAT. PK.
San Diego
Tijuana
5
101
80
50
395
680
280
99
36
58
15
40
10
8
© American Map Corporation

ALASKA!

These are the last two states to join the U.S. of A.— a string of islands and a giant chunk of ice. They are state number 49, Alaska, and the big five-o, Hawaii!

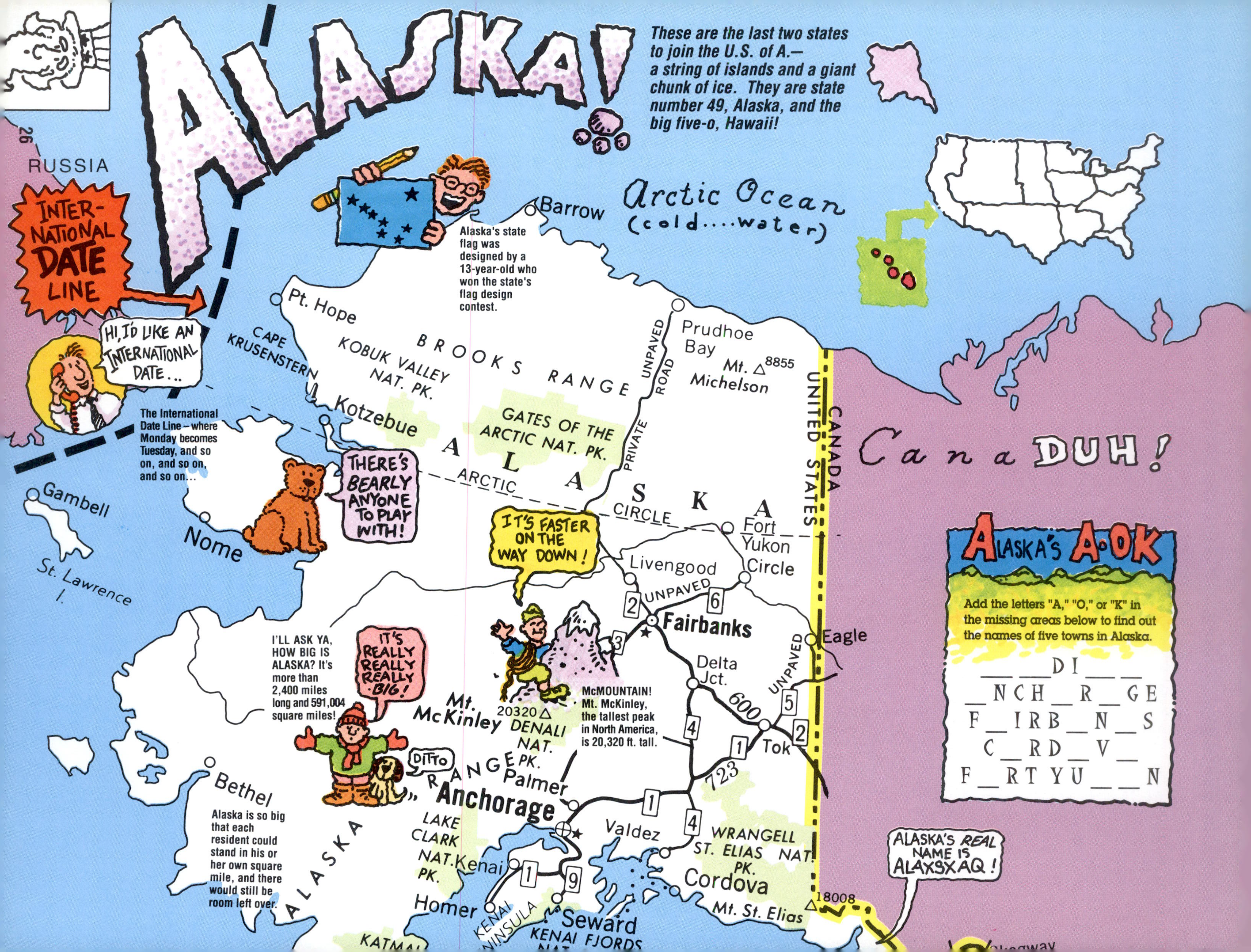

ALASKA'S A-OK

Add the letters "A," "O," or "K" in the missing areas below to find out the names of five towns in Alaska.

__ __ D I __ __

__ N C H __ R __ G E

F __ I R B __ N __ S

C __ R D __ V __

F __ R T Y U __ __ N

MORE ALASKA THIS-A-WAY
ALASKA PENINSULA
ANIAKCHAK
Kodiak
KODIAK I.
LAUGHABLE LAWS
In Hawaii, it is illegal to insert pennies into one's ears.
ICY YOU!
Circle the animals you might see if you were to look out through the window of an Alaskan igloo.
Reindeer FLAMINGO Hawk
Brown Bear Camel WHALE
POLAR BEAR Sea Lion Giraffe
FLAMINGO Kangaroo PENGUIN
GLACIER BAY NAT. PK.
ADMIRALTY ISLAND
Sitka
SITKA NAT. HIST. PK.
MUK LUKS
JUNEAU
CANADA
UNITED STATES
FERRY
Ketchikan
MISTY FJORDS
OUR SPELLING BEES ARE A BREEZE!
VACANCY
AEHIKLMNPOWU
The Hawaiian language has only 12 letters.
"O"
IT'S JUST NOT FAIR
Big fish, little name.
Little fish, big name. Weird.
HOMOMOMONUKUNUKUAGUK
The Hawaiian Islands are made up of 122 islands, but Hawaiians only live on seven.
KAUAI
Waimea
Niihau
Kapaa
Lihue
OAHU
Wahiawa
Kailua
HONOLULU
MOLOKAI
Maunaloa
Kaunakakai
Wailuku
MAUI
HALEAKALA NAT PARK
Lana City
Lanai
Kahoolawe
I JUST LAVA THIS BEACH!
TINY BUBBLES
WHO KNOWS VOLCANOES
Alaska and Hawaii have volcanoes that really blow. Both states are on the Pacific Rim, a part of the globe that is filled with these fiery mountains. Can you identify two volcanoes? Unscramble their names below, then find them on the map.
AANUM OAL
ANAMU AKE
HAWAII
The black sand at Kamoamoa Black Sand Beach, on the island of Hawaii, is actually small grains of lava.
Honokaa
Mauna Kea
13796
HAWAII
Mauna Loa
13680
Hilo
Pahoa
Pahala
HAWAII VOLCANOES NAT. PK.
Kamoamoa Black Sand Beach
Naalehu
© American Map Corporation
When measured from the ocean floor, Mauna Loa is the world's largest mountain – 30,000 feet!
Popular Hawaiian kid activities are surfing, hula dancing, POG collecting and seeing Don Ho! (Don who?)
Major Hawaiian crops are sugar cane, coffee, macadamia nuts, and pineapple.
Coffee

NATIONAL NONSENSE

Highway "Highjinks" & Coast 2 Coast Chaos

Nicknack.....

Cities have nicknames, just like people. Look at these nicknames, then unscramble their real names.

The Windy City ____________ HCIGOCA
The Big Apple ____________ WEN KOYR
The Motor City ____________ TROIEDT
The Big Easy ____________ EWN LEORASN
Beantown ____________ TOONSB

Answers: Chicago, Illinois; New York, New York; Detroit, Michigan; New Orleans, Louisiana; Boston, Massachusetts.

Hungry

Check out these tasty spots named after some favorite foods. You'll have an especially flavorful time if you go to Texas.

Orange, Texas
Coke, Texas
Ding Dong, Texas
Sandwich, Illinois

Plum, Pennsylvania
Coffeeville, Alabama
Two Egg, Florida

Map-Rap

We're going
hip hoppin' cross the U.S.A.
Hope I don't hurl
in the car today!
Transportation. Destinations.
Geographical navigations.
I've got a hungry
fascination for information!
Gonna learn some weird things
'bout the whole darn nation,
Cuz I'm mappin' and
rappin' on my vacation!

Map TAP.......

Here's a tip-top game for two mappers. To play, player one opens the atlas, picks out a specific location and says, "I see a (city, state, park, whatever)," then, gives the first and last letters of the location. Player two taps his or her finger across the map while the other player gives "hot" or "cold" clues. When player two identifies the location, switch places and start again.

DOME ROAM

Solve the clues to identify these super stadiums:

1. Where the striped-cats from Detroit play baseball.
2. The Chicago Cubs chew a lot of spearmint gum here.
3. You have to climb way up to reach this amphitheater in Denver, Colorado.
4. This San Francisco stadium is home of a slow and steady burn.

Answers: Tiger Stadium, Wrigley Field, Mile High Stadium, Candlestick Park

It ain't Disney World

(BUT IT'S ALMOST AS FUN)

Wanna get wacky and have a really good time? Here are some of our favorite off-the-wall, off-the-beaten-path picks:

1. *Frog Festival - Rayne, Louisiana*
2. *Gilroy Garlic Festival - Gilroy, California*
3. *Junior Chili Cook-Off - San Marcos, Texas*
4. *Junior World Championship Duck Calling Contest - Stuttgart, Arkansas*
5. *Lakeview Sled Dog Races - Lakeview, Oregon*

COLLEGE CAN BE A REAL ANIMAL HOUSE

You have to be a real beast to play college football! These teams are definite proof of that. Take a tour through this wild college football zoo:

YOUNGSTOWN STATE
PENGUINS

TEXAS CHRISTIAN
HORNED FROGS

TEMPLE
OWLS

BOSTON UNIVERSITY
TERRIERS

MONTANA
GRIZZLIES

DELAWARE
BLUE HENS

MONTANA STATE
BOBCATS

UNIVERSITY OF MICHIGAN
WOLVERINES

ATLAS, I've FOUND YOU!

A MAP-MAGICAL STORY YOU MAKE UP YOURSELF!

Fill in the blanks again and again to make your own crazy, cross-country tale.

While driving to ________ (state) to visit my ________ (adjective) ________ (relative's name), we stopped at a rest-stop because my ________ (relative) ________ (gross verb (past tense)) all over the back seat! It smelled like a ________ (adjective) ________ (animal)! At the rest-stop, I took our dog ________ (name) for a walk. He saw a ________ (noun) and ran away. He followed the critter into the restaurant and tripped a ________ (adjective) lady carrying a tray of ________ (messy food). Luckily, I caught him before he bumped into a really ________ (adjective) truck driver. I was so ________ (emotion), I yelled, "Atlas, I've found you!"

BIG ONE BINGO
Stockton, California, approximately 50 miles south of Sacramento, also felt the big jolt.

SASQUATCH WATCH
Sasquatch is hiding in the covered wagon in Oregon.

LIFE IN THE PITS
Saber-toothed tiger, giant sloth.

MOUNTAIN

BUFFALO BLUFF
The buffalo on the right is different in these five ways: no feet, smile, right horn crooked, tail down, no spot on back.

CAPITAL CAPTURE
The wild west train robber is Butch Cassidy.

SHEEP SEARCH
The six sheep can be found at these coordinates: E-5, K-9, F-11, M/N-12/13, E/F-13, I/J-13.

GLACIER GOOFS
The following items don't belong in the ice cube: watch, sock, video game control, baseball, and sandwich.

SPUD PUZZLER
You'll need 2 1/3 french fries to measure the approximate 230 mile distance from Boise to Pocatello. (Eat the other 2/3.)

PLAINS

MAPMANIA
There are five dinosaur bones hidden throughout this region.

TORNADO TWISTER
Take I-135 to I-70, turn left, go to Rt.83. Take Rt.83 north to North Platt. Turn right and go east on I-80 to Omaha.

ROADKILL SCRAMBLE
Skunk, Possum, Raccoon

REST-STOP ROUND-UP
These tacky items can be found in these states:
Postcard, Kansas
Troll doll, North Dakota
Baseball cap, Kansas
Mug, North Dakota
Snow globe, South Dakota

CITY SEARCH
Valentine, Nebraska
Wichita, Kansas

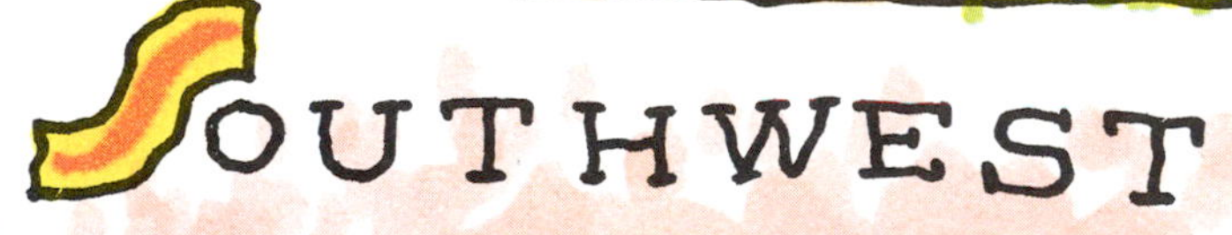

MAPMANIA
K-15 = Houston, Texas
E-7 = Santa Fe, New Mexico
E- 13 = Oklahoma City, Oklahoma

SANTA FE, OLE
ASLAS = SALSA
OSLTRITAL = TORTILLAS
CELGMAAUO = GUACAMOLE

ICY YOU
reindeer,
hawk,
brown bear,
polar bear,
sea lion
(gotcha! - penguins are only found in Antarctica)

ALASKA! IS A.O.K.
Kodiak,
Anchorage,
Fairbanks,
Cordova,
Fort Yukon.

HAWAII

WHO KNOWS VOLCANOES
Mauna Loa
Mauna Kea

SOLUTIONS
NORTH CENTRAL
BOGUS BILLBOARD
Appleton, Wisconsin
CAPITAL COORDINATES
St. Paul, Minnesota = I-6
Lansing, Michigan = K/L-15
Madison, Wisconsin = K/L-10
WHAT A BUNCH OF FLAKES
The two highlighted flakes are identical and can be found in Battle Creek, Michigan.
ROADSIDE RALLY
PEACE PIPE, Minnesota.
CHERRIES, Michigan.
JUMP ROPE, Wisconsin.
FREAKY FINDS
The whale skeleton is in western Vermont at I-11.
LOBSTER LOOKOUT
There are six lobsters hidden on the map.
New England
GEOGRAFFITI TIME
The first lollipop was made in New Haven, Connecticut.
MidWEST
MAPMANIA – It will be 4:00 p.m. when you arrive in Indianapolis.
RACE TO INDY – Davenport, Iowa and Hannibal, Missouri are both approximately 250 miles away from Indianapolis.
CORNY CODES – Sweet corn, popcorn, feed corn.
WHO'S YOUR HOOSIER?
K-15 = Evansville
E-18 = Fort Wayne
H-17 = Shelbyville
MIDATLANTIC
GROUSE ME OUT
The five ruffled grouses can be found at these coordinates: I/J-3/4, L-8/9, G-9, F/G-13/14, E-16.
MAPMANIA
The other historical monuments are Fort McHenry and the Washington Monument.
ROADSIDE RALLY
F P C A I T C A C
T O H H S D B A H
C A O A L M T L P
D L C S L A G A F
S E O N A C L O V
E Y L V B M O C S
I F A P T B V G L
N O T R O A A N H
O T E A O L F E W
P E K N F S U F I
S R E T S Y O M Y
SOUTHEAST
SNAKE EYES There are 15 slimy snakes.
THE WRIGHT FLIGHTS
Kitty Hawk to Raleigh 200 miles
Kitty Hawk to Charlotte 330 miles
Kitty Hawk to Winston Salem 290 miles
SOUTH CENTRAL
The King: Elvis Presley
The Spring: Hot Springs National Park
The Real Thing: Coca-Cola
BLUEGRASS BINGO
B-15 = Washington, D.C.
I-12/13 = Florence, South Carolina
N-8 = Tifton, Georgia
G-2/3 = Jackson, Tennessee
O-8/9 = Valdosta, Georgia
Florida
GATOR BRIGADE
Take I-75 to I-4 and go east toward Daytona. Continue north on I-95. Turn left at Jacksonville and take I-10 to Tallahassee.
TRICKY TREES
The first tree in the first row and the last tree in the second row are identical.
GEOGRAPHY EXAM ANSWERS
How could we possibly know the answers to your geography exam? Even if we did, we wouldn't tell you!
CAPITAL CAPER Tallahassee is the capital of Florida. Some other words you can make include: tall, hall, seal, lease, last, alas, and atlas!
FLOWER POWER
Florida's state flower is the Orange Blossom.

YOUR Trip... YOUR turn
my 5 favorite places to Visit
1
2
3
4
5
PLEASE
don't ever make me go back to...
The HOTTEST place I've ever been...
The Coldest!
Phew! the smelliest town is...
Maybe it's Just Dad
I almost got carsick in...
(o.k., so I really did get carsick)
My Parents got really lost in...
we're not LOST!
This is ABSOLUTELY the end of the ROAD...
STOP